MODERN WORLD NATIONS

AFGHANISTAN
AUSTRIA
BAHRAIN
BERMUDA
CHINA
CROATIA
CUBA
EGYPT
ENGLAND
ETHIOPIA
REPUBLIC OF GEORGIA
GERMANY
KUWAIT
IRAN
IRAQ
ISRAEL
MEXICO
NEW ZEALAND
PAKISTAN
RUSSIA
SAUDI ARABIA
SCOTLAND
SOUTH KOREA
UKRAINE

Ethiopia

Carol Ann Gillespie
Grove City College

Series Consulting Editor
Charles F. Gritzner
South Dakota State University

A Haights Cross Communications Company

Philadelphia

Frontispiece: Flag of Ethiopia

Cover: Blue Nile Falls near Bahir Dar, Ethiopia

CHELSEA HOUSE PUBLISHERS

VP, New Product Development Sally Cheney
Director of Production Kim Shinners
Creative Manager Takeshi Takahashi
Manufacturing Manager Diann Grasse

Staff for ETHIOPIA

Editor Lee Marcott
Production Editor Jaimie Winkler
Picture Researcher Pat Holl
Cover and Series Designer Takeshi Takahashi
Layout 21st Century Publishing and Communications, Inc.

A Haights Cross Communications Company

http://www.chelseahouse.com

First Printing

1 3 5 7 9 8 6 4 2

Library of Congress Cataloging-in-Publication Data

Gillespie, Carol Ann.
   Ethiopia / Carol Ann Gillespie.
      p. cm. — (Modern world nations)
Summary: Describes the history, geography, government, economy, people, and
culture of Ethiopia.
Includes index.
   ISBN 0-7910-6780-7 — ISBN 0-7910-7106-5 (pbk.)
   1. Ethiopia—Juvenile literature. [1. Ethiopia.] I. Title. II. Series.
DT373 .G55 2002
963—dc21
                                                        2002011451

Table of Contents

Ethiopia

Ethiopia is a land of many contrasts. Its landscape varies from barren desert to the lush green of the Ethiopian Plateau. Much of Ethiopia receives ample rainfall, although some regions must rely on seasonal rainfall.

Introducing Ethiopia

E thiopia shocked the world in 1974 when photographs of the country's horrible famines were published. Many people got the mistaken notion that Ethiopia was nothing but a vast, dry desert where food was unavailable for either people or beasts. Nothing could be further from the truth. Much of Ethiopia receives ample rainfall, in some places distributed all through the year, although a few places must rely on seasonal rains. Because much of the country is highly elevated, large areas range in temperature from cool to cold throughout the year. In Ethiopia, temperature depends more on the elevation of the land than on the tropical latitude.

But, it is true that large areas of Africa suffer from scant and often unreliable rainfall, resulting in frequent drought. Ethiopia is no exception. It is also one of the poorest nations on Earth. The country faces many difficulties in providing for the needs of its 65 million people. Nevertheless, Ethiopia has a rich history and an amazing diversity of people, climates, land features, and ecosystems. Until 1974, Ethiopia had an unbroken line of kings and emperors dating back to biblical times. It would be sad if all people ever thought about when considering Ethiopia was famine. There are many more exciting things to know about this fascinating country.

ETHIOPIA—CRADLE OF HUMANKIND?

Archaeologists (scientists who study ancient human life) believe that the earliest ancestors of modern humans came from equatorial east Africa—perhaps from some place in or near the Great Rift Valley. This huge trench-like landform—Africa's largest and most distinctive geologic feature—runs southwest to northeast across Ethiopia. During the twentieth century, it yielded many clues about the origin of humankind. Our oldest anthropoid (primate) ancestor—named *Homo ramidus afarensis*—may have lived in what is now Ethiopia some 4.4 million years ago. In 1975, archaeologists excavating sites in the Awash River valley discovered 3.5 million-year-old fossil skeletons. They named these remains *Australopithecus afarensis*. These earliest known hominids—the best known of which is named Lucy—stood upright, lived in groups, and had adapted to life in open areas rather than in forests. They are believed to be the earliest ancestors of modern humans, and they lived in Ethiopia.

HOME TO THE ARK OF THE COVENANT?

The Ark of the Covenant—the chest believed to hold the stone tablets on which the Ten Commandments were written—is the most sacred relic of the Bible's Old Testament. According to ancient legend, the Ark of the Covenant found its way to Ethiopia centuries before the birth of Jesus Christ. By legend, it was Menelik, son of King Solomon and the Queen of Sheba, who brought the Ark to Ethiopia during the fifth century B.C. One of the African continent's oldest churches, St. Mary of Zion, was built in Axum to house the Ark of the Covenant. In the

Many scientists believe that the first ancestors of modern humans lived in Ethiopia. Archaeologists Donald C. Johnson (left) and Tim White (right) contributed to this theory when they found fossils in Ethiopia of the most primitive species of ape yet known.

early 1530s, invading Muslim armies sacked the church and the Ethiopians moved the sacred relic to a hidden location to keep it safe. When Ethiopia was once again at peace, the Ark was brought back to Axum and installed in a newly built St. Mary's Church near the one that had been destroyed.

Today, this religious treasure reportedly is kept in a small chapel in Axum, the ancient city that was once Ethiopia's capital. One of Ethiopia's former emperors, Haile Selassie, had the chapel built in Axum in 1965 to house the Ark. Selassie took special interest in its safe housing and preservation because he was the 225th direct descendant of Menelik. No one is allowed to enter the chapel except the monk who is responsible for guarding it. Anyone who might attempt to do so would be killed.

EARLY CHRISTIAN KINGDOM

Ethiopia is one of the world's oldest Christian nations. We know about the conversion of Ethiopia to Christianity from the writings of a fourth-century theologian, Rufinius. He wrote about a Christian merchant who was on a trade voyage to India. On the return journey through the Red Sea, his ship was seized off the Ethiopian coast in an act of revenge against the Roman Empire, which had broken a treaty with the local people. The Christian merchant was killed in the fighting. Two young boys who were making the trip with him survived, however, and were taken to the king of Axum, capital of ancient Ethiopia.

The king, it is said, gave the boys positions of great honor in his kingdom. One of the boys, Frumentius, became very power-ful and influential in the Axumite kingdom over the years. He welcomed foreign travelers who were Christians and invited them to build places for prayer. He gave them everything they needed to accomplish this task—including land, building materials, and labor. In this way, Frumentius promoted the establishment of Christianity in Ethiopia. The Patriarch of Alexandria honored Frumentius by naming him the first Christian bishop of Ethiopia. Alexandria was a great center of Christianity in Egypt during that time. Frumentius was respon-sible for many people converting to Christianity, including the king of Axum himself in the year A.D. 331. In those days, kings and rulers put important symbols of their reign on the country's coins. Ethiopia has some of the first coins in the world to bear the cross as a symbol of Christianity. Today, some 1700 years later, Eastern Orthodoxy (the most common form of Christianity in Eastern Europe) continues to be Ethiopia's most common Christian faith. Religion, however, is just one of many fascinating aspects of Ethiopia's heritage.

THE ORIGINS OF COFFEE

One of the world's most popular drinks—coffee—also came from Ethiopia. An Ethiopian legend tells of a shepherd who noticed that his flock of goats was very restless and did not sleep at night after grazing on bushes that were heavy with red beans. Later, the shepherd told some monks about the beans,

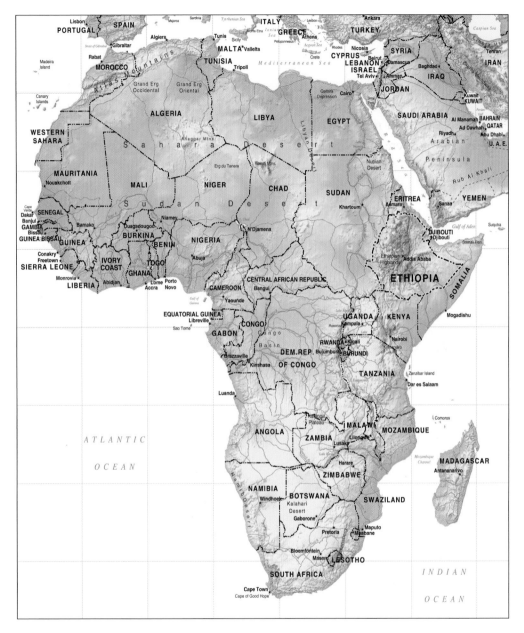

Ethiopia occupies the Horn of Africa—the peninsula of eastern Africa that juts into the Indian Ocean. This highland and the adjacent areas occupy the horn and much of the region lies at elevations above 10,000 feet (3,050 meters). Ethiopia borders Eritrea on the north and northeast, Djibouti and Somalia on the east, Kenya to the south, and Sudan to the west.

and the monks used them so they could stay awake for all-night prayer sessions.

It is not known whether this legend is based on any truth. However, it is known that coffee was first grown in the forested highlands of southern Ethiopia (in the region of Kaffa), where wild varieties still grow. The Greek writer Homer mentioned coffee in the seventh century B.C. This suggests that knowledge of this unusual plant and its properties had spread far beyond its place of origin. Actual cultivation of these plants is believed to have occurred as early as A.D. 575. It is known that around this time, the ancient Ethiopians were exporting coffee to nearby Yemen. Coffee bushes flourished in Yemen, and soon the entire Arab world was consuming the new beverage. Today, coffee is Ethiopia's largest export, generating about 60 percent of all the country's export earnings. Nearly a quarter of the country's people directly or indirectly depend on coffee for their livelihood.

LAND OF GREAT POTENTIAL

By African standards, Ethiopia is a country with great potential. Much of the country is blessed with fertile soil and adequate rainfall. Because of its high average elevation, much of the country has moderate temperatures. This proud land also has a history of independence—it is the only country on the African continent that was never fully colonized by a European power. Economically, farmers can grow a variety of grains, including wheat, corn, and millet. Coffee grows well on southern slopes. Herders can raise cattle, sheep, and goats in most parts of the country. In addition, Ethiopia contains several valuable minerals, including gold and platinum.

Unlike most other African countries, Ethiopia has been able to maintain contacts with the outside world for centuries because of its resources. Since ancient times, Ethiopian traders exchanged gold, ivory, musk, and wild animal hides for luxury goods such as silk and velvet. By the late nineteenth century, coffee had become one of Ethiopia's most important cash crops. In spite of its great riches, however, Ethiopia never became a great trading nation. Most Ethiopians despised traders. They looked up to and wanted to be priests and warriors, professions that were more highly respected. As a result, other ethnic groups, such as the Arabs, Greeks, and Armenians, set up business in Ethiopia and carried on most of Ethiopia's trade with the outside world. Arabs settled in the interior of Ethiopia and took over most commercial trade.

Today, Ethiopia's economy is based on agriculture, which accounts for half of the gross domestic product (GDP). Agriculture is difficult, though, because of frequent periods of drought and poor cultivation practices. Every year, millions of Ethiopians need food assistance just to feed their families. A recent war with Eritrea (a country in North Africa that was once part of Ethiopia) has forced the country to spend precious money on the military instead of development. Nevertheless, Ethiopia has great potential to become more than just a treasure trove of artifacts and history.

Ethiopia is blessed with a wealth of human resources. Perhaps surprisingly, many of the world's people first became aware of some Ethiopians' excellence at long-distance running. Ethiopia has produced a number of world-class long-distance runners. Gezehegne Abera, the best marathon runner in the world, comes from Ethiopia. In Addis Ababa, the capital of Ethiopia, portraits of five great Ethiopian long-distance champions adorn the stadium scoreboard. At the 2000 Olympics in Sydney, Australia, Ethiopia won seven medals—four of them gold—in track and field, more than any other African nation. Despite this success, Ethiopia, as you will learn from the pages of this book, is a country with many problems. If these problems can be overcome, however, the country has the potential to become a leader among African nations.

Ethiopia's major land feature is the massive highland complex of mountains and plateaus divided by the Great Rift Valley, which is surrounded by lowlands along the country's edge. This aerial view shows how the valley bisects this mountainous plateau.

2

Ethiopia's Natural Landscapes

E thiopia occupies most of the Horn of Africa—the penin-
sula of eastern Africa that juts prominently into the
Indian Ocean. The country covers approximately 435,000
square miles, an area about the size of the states of Texas, New
Mexico, and Arizona combined. It is interesting to note that
many sources give different numbers for the size of Ethiopia.
One reason for these differences is the frequent change caused
by Ethiopia's ongoing territorial conflicts with its neighbors.
Eritrea borders the country on the north and northeast. Small
Djibouti is tucked into its eastern border. Somalia is its largest
neighbor on the east. Kenya to the south and Sudan to the west
are Ethiopia's other neighbors.

FEATURES OF THE LAND

Ethiopia's major land feature is a massive highland complex of mountains and plateaus divided by the Great Rift Valley and surrounded by lowlands along much of the country's edge. These highlands are called the Ethiopian Plateau. The Great Rift Valley bisects this mountainous plateau, dividing it into northwestern and southeastern highland regions. The northwestern highlands are larger and more rugged. In the northwest, the region is further subdivided into northern and southern sections by the valley of the Blue Nile River.

Much of the Ethiopian Plateau averages 5,500 feet (1,676 meters) in elevation—about a mile above sea level. Actual elevations range between 3,000 to 9,000 feet (roughly 1,000 to 3,000 meters). Volcanic peaks rise here and there above the plateau surface. The country's highest point is the 15,571-foot (4,746-meter) Ras Dashen Terara, which towers over the surrounding landscape northeast of Gonder. Ethiopia's historical core lies in the northernmost portion of the plateau, which is the location of the ancient kingdom of Axum.

Ethiopia's modern capital city of Addis Ababa is located in the center of the country on the edge of the central plateau. Rapidly flowing streams, fed by mountain rains and melting snow, have eroded many deep, steep-sided valleys in the plateau surface. These streams are not suitable for navigation, but are potential sources of hydroelectric power and water for irrigation.

North of Addis Ababa, the plateau is covered with a mixture of towering mountains and deep chasms, or gorges, that contain a wide variety of native vegetation. The plateau contains the Chercher and Aranna mountain ranges. Ethiopians refer to this central tableland and the rugged mountains surrounding it as a plateau. This startles many tourists when they first come to Ethiopia, because the terrain is anything but flat, as plateaus usually are. The Ethiopians call the few mountainous peaks that are flat *ambas*.

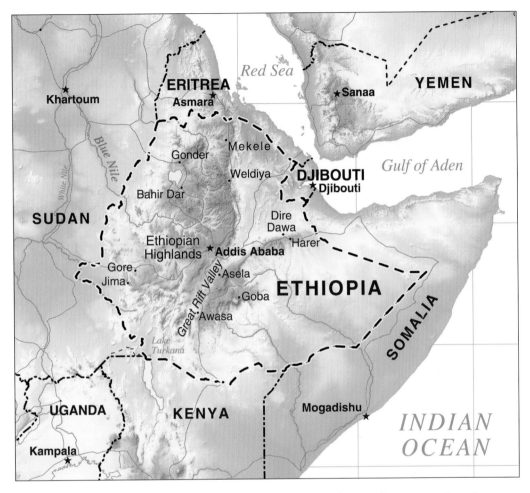

The Great Rift Valley divides the Ethiopian Plateau into northwestern and southeastern highland regions. The northwestern highlands are more rugged. In the northwest, the region is split into a northern and southern section by the valley of the Blue Nile River.

Southwest of Addis Ababa, the plateau is rugged, but at a slightly lower elevation than the northern section. Southeast of Addis Ababa, the plateau slopes gently to the southeast. The land there is rocky desert and is sparsely populated.

The Great Rift Valley forms a third region. It is part of a huge fault system that extends from the Jordan River Valley in the Middle East southward to the mouth of the Zambezi River in Mozambique. The portion of the Great Rift Valley that runs through central Ethiopia is marked in the north by the funnel-shaped saline plain called the Denakil (Dallol) Depression. To the south, the Great Rift Valley becomes a deep trench that slices through the central plateau. A chain of fairly large lakes dots the southern half of the Ethiopian segment of the Great Rift Valley. Some of the lakes are freshwater and are fed by springs from the east. Other lakes contain salts and other minerals and their waters are of no use to humans.

To the north, the Great Rift Valley stretches out into the Denakil (Dallol) Depression. This is a large basin that is shaped like a triangle and reaches an elevation of approximately 410 feet (125 meters) below sea level in places. The Denakil Depression is one of the hottest and driest places on earth. A narrow strip of coastal hills rims its northeastern edge. These hills border a hot, dry, treeless strip of coast approximately 80 kilometers wide. The coastal hills drain inland into salty lakes. As the water evaporates, salt deposits are left behind (as occurs on the floor of Utah's Bonneville Salt Flats). Salt has long been mined from these lakebeds.

Small volcanoes, hot springs, and numerous deep gorges indicate that large portions of the Ethiopian plateau are geologically unstable. Many active volcanoes surround the Denakil Depression, and hot springs and steaming fissures are found in other northern parts of the Great Rift Valley. In recent memory, several small earthquakes have also been recorded in the area.

RIVERS AND LAKES

All of Ethiopia's rivers originate in the highlands and flow outward in many directions through deep gorges. The Blue Nile is Ethiopia's largest river. It rises at Lake Tana and flows in a general southeasterly direction, before looping westward and then northwestward as it passes into Sudan. On its journey, the river cuts through one of the world's largest gorges, which is

Ethiopia has some of the largest salt deposits in the world. The area of the Denakil Depression holds lakebeds from which salt is mined.

longer and wider than the Grand Canyon. It also plunges over spectacular waterfalls called *Tis Issat*, or "water that smokes," by native Ethiopians. Eventually, the Blue Nile joins the White Nile at Khartoum in neighboring Sudan. Waters of the White Nile contribute some two-thirds of the Nile's total volume below (north of) Khartoum.

Three of the rivers that originate in the Ethiopian highlands—the Blue Nile, the Tekeze, and the Baro—account for over half of Ethiopia's water outflow. The Awash River flows through the northern half of the Great Rift Valley. Several dams built on the river by the Ethiopian government generate hydroelectric power. Electricity produced by these dams is used to irrigate major commercial plantations. The Awash River flows east and disappears in the salty lakes near the border with Djibouti. The Genale and Shebele rivers and their tributaries drain the southeastern part of Ethiopia, and the Omo River drains the southwest.

South of Addis Ababa, more than a dozen lakes occupy deep trenches on the floor of the Great Rift Valley. The floor of Lake Shalla, the deepest of Ethiopia's lakes, lies almost 900 feet below its surface. Water in hot springs found along the shore of Lake Shalla is so hot that villagers boil their grain there. Many of the lakes teem with fish, and birds flock to their waters and shores by the million. Lake Chamo is said to offer some of the best crocodile viewing in all of Africa.

Travelers to the region often describe the scenery surrounding several of the lakes as some of the most spectacular in the world. Tourist hotels, lodges, and camping facilities accommodate travelers to many of the lakes. Certainly, this region offers tremendous potential for future tourist development. In the north, Lake Tana, the source of the Blue Nile River, occupies a broad but shallow basin at an elevation of more than a mile above sea level. Measuring some 40 by 50 miles (64 by 80 kilometers) at its widest points, Tana occupies an area of about 1,220 square miles (3,159 square kilometers) and is Ethiopia's largest water body.

WEATHER AND CLIMATE

Ethiopia's weather and climate are largely a result of two conditions—its position in Africa's tropical zone, and its varied topography. The country has three climate zones, each of which is based on elevation. These are the *dega*, or cool zone, located above 8,000 feet (2,438 meters); the *weina dega*, or temperate zone, located between 5,000 and 8,000 feet (1,524 and 2,438 meters); and the *kolla*, or hot zone, lying at elevations below 5,000 feet.

The cool zone, or *dega*, is found at higher elevations in much of the northwestern plateau region and in several smaller areas in the eastern and central mountains. The terrain lies at an elevation of over 8,000 feet. Average daily temperatures are cool, with highs that range from freezing at highest elevations to the fifties Fahrenheit at the lower margins. March, April, and May are the warmest months in this zone. Here, afternoons cool down quickly and nights are usually cold. Most of the year, freezing temperatures with light frosts occur during the night. At high elevations, snow falls frequently and may remain on the ground throughout the year.

The temperate zone, or *weina dega*, is found at lower levels of the plateau at elevations between approximately 5,000 and 8,000 feet. This zone has been called a "land of perpetual spring." This area does not experience either high or low extremes in temperature. Rather, temperatures fall into a spring-like 50° to 70° F (10° to 21° C) range. Nighttime temperatures can drop toward freezing and afternoon highs can get quite warm. Even so, conditions never reach the extremes found in the higher or lower climatic zones.

The hot zone, or *kolla*, lies at elevations lower than 5,000 feet. This area includes the Denakil and outlying areas. It also includes the deep tropical valleys of the Blue Nile and Tekeze rivers, and the country's borders with Sudan and Kenya. Humidity is usually high in these tropical valleys, making the temperatures seem even higher. The average annual daytime temperature is about 80° F, but the temperatures vary widely in this climate zone of Ethiopia.

People often like to know weather extremes, such as the highest and lowest temperatures ever recorded in a particular country or place. This information is difficult to obtain for Ethiopia. Certainly the lowest temperatures would fall well below freezing, and perhaps below zero degrees Fahrenheit at the highest elevations. The hottest temperatures, on the other hand, occur in the Denakil Depression. Official records indicate that afternoon temperatures frequently reach 130° F (54° C) in the shade. This blistering desert holds one world record that no other place can come close to matching (or would want to)—from 1960 to 1966, the annual average temperature was a scorching 94° F (34° C).

Variations in rainfall throughout Ethiopia are the result of two major factors: differences in elevation and seasonal changes in the atmospheric pressure systems that control the prevailing wind systems. It is for these reasons that several regions receive rainfall throughout most of the year, but precipitation is seasonal in other areas. Rainfall is always meager in the lowlands, where arid desert conditions prevail.

During the winter months, a high-pressure system located over eastern Siberia in northern Russia produces winds that blow across the Red Sea. These northeasterly winds bring rain to the coastal plains and steep eastern slope of Eritrea. They are cool and dry, however, and bring very little rain to Ethiopia. Late spring and summer winds that originate over the Indian Ocean and blow into eastern Africa have a strong seasonal effect on much of Ethiopia. The higher elevations of the interior highlands cause the moisture-laden winds to drop much of their precipitation during the period from spring to mid-September.

The main rainy season is usually preceded by a brief period in April and May of light rains, known as *balg*. These rains are created by the convergence of northeast and southeast winds. After the *balg* rains, there is a short period of hot, dry weather. By the middle of June, violent thunderstorms become a daily occurrence in the humid parts of the country. In the southwest, precipitation is more abundant and more evenly distributed. Ethiopia's relative humidity and rainfall generally decrease from south to north. It is greatest in the southwest, light in the Great Rift Valley and eastern desert region of Ogaden, and rare in the parched Denakil Depression.

TREES OF ETHIOPIA

In terms of natural vegetation, Ethiopia appears to be heading toward an environmental catastrophe. In the late nineteenth century, approximately 30 percent of the country was covered with forest. As the population grew, however, the demand for firewood and agricultural land greatly increased. Today, Ethiopia's forested areas have dwindled to less than 3 percent of the country's area. The northern part of the highlands is almost totally devoid of trees. Most of the remaining forests are found in remote areas of the southern and southwestern highlands. Some of these include coniferous forests, found at elevations above 5,000 feet (1,524 km).

Lumber from the coniferous forests is important to the construction industry. The broadleaf evergreen forests furnish timber that is used in construction and in the production of plywood. Of greatest importance to Ethiopians—most of whom are very poor—is the use of wood as a major source of firewood and charcoal. Wood is their only source of fuel. Until the country's economy improves and people can afford other means of heating and cooking, forestlands will continue to suffer.

Certain species of trees are of special economic significance. Two species that grow in the lowland deserts produce resins from which frankincense and myrrh are derived. A species of acacia found in several parts of Ethiopia is a source of gum arabic used in the manufacture of adhesives, medicines, candy, and other products. Eucalyptus trees also are common in parts of the country. This useful species was introduced during the late nineteenth century from its native Australia. Because of its unusually rapid growth and ability to survive in semi-arid conditions, the tree became very popular in urban areas. In rural parts of the country, it has become an important cash crop for farmers. Eucalyptus wood is used for many things, including telephone poles, tool handles, furniture, and firewood. Fiberboard and particleboard are also made from large quantities of eucalyptus.

Before 1974, about half of the forestland was privately owned or claimed, and the government held the other half. Then, in 1975, the government took control of all forestland and sawmills, most of which were in the southern part of Ethiopia. The government controlled all harvesting of forestland. Individuals had to obtain permits from local peasant associations to cut trees. This measure encouraged illegal logging and accelerated the destruction of Ethiopia's remaining forests. To ensure that conservation activity conformed to government policies on land use, reforestation programs were organized through the Ministry of Agriculture or district offices. These offices planned, coordinated, and monitored all work. Local peasant associations did not have decision-making authority.

Through reforestation programs millions of seedlings were planted in community forests throughout Ethiopia. Several non-governmental organizations (NGOs) supplemented the government's efforts to replenish Ethiopia's forests. However, some critics claim that the systems develop communal resources at the expense of private needs. For this reason, reforestation programs did not perform well or reap good results in Ethiopia. Seedling survival rates were low: only 5 to 20 percent in some areas, and up to 40 percent in others. The planted seedlings suffered from inadequate care, drought, and premature cutting by peasants. Ethiopia instituted a plan in 1990 called the Ethiopian Forestry Action Plan (EFAP). Its goals are to improve forestry conservation, increase public participation in reforestation projects, and prevent further depletion of existing forest resources.

WILD PLANTS AND FAMINE FOODS

Rural people of Ethiopia have a deep knowledge about the use of wild plants. They know what kinds of wild plants can be consumed during times of drought, war, and other hardships. Elders and other knowledgeable community members are the chief sources, or "reservoirs," of plant lore. Wild-food consumption is still very common in rural areas of Ethiopia, especially among children. Some of the most common wild plant fruits eaten by Ethiopian children are those from *Ficus* (figs), *Carissa edulis* (plums), and *Rosa abyssinica* (rose) plant species.

The consumption of wild plants seems more common and widespread in food shortage areas. There, a wide range of species is consumed. Certain plants are called "famine-foods" and are consumed only in times of food stress. Therefore, they play a vital role as indicators of possible famine conditions. Ethiopians know about the importance of wild plants to their daily diet. They also are aware of possible health hazards, such as stomach irritation that occasionally occurs after the consumption of certain wild plants.

In parts of southern Ethiopia, the consumption of wild-food plants is one of the main local survival strategies in severe food shortages. Increased consumption of wild plants helps the people cope with food shortages caused by long periods of drought. The key to this survival strategy is to collect and eat wild plants in uncultivated lowland areas such as bush, forest, and pastureland. People also have domesticated (deliberately planted and cared for) many of these native trees and plants for home consumption or medicinal use.

The southern part of the country is Ethiopia's greatest source of biodiversity and wild plant use. For example, the Konso people of southern Ethiopia are well known for their strong work ethic and their sophisticated agricultural system. However, beginning in 1996, they were stricken by what proved to be a drought that would last for years. They have experienced repeated severe harvest losses and even complete crop failures. Even so, up until June 1999, most Konso people managed to cope with these harsh climatic conditions and survived by increasing their consumption of wild plants. Damaged, reduced, and even lost crop harvests have been partly compensated by the collection of wild foods. Unfortunately, three severe years with only meager harvests and yet another harvest failure in 1999 were just too much for many Konso people. Konso is an ecologically fragile area, despite the people's incredible efforts to protect and conserve the local environment.

Many plants thought of as "famine-foods" are not eaten regularly because of certain undesirable characteristics. They may have thorns, a bad taste, be complicated to prepare, or cause undesirable physical complaints, such as diarrhea, stomach pain, or intoxication. For example, the fruits of *Dobera glabra*—the Konso people's major drought indicator plant—are edible. However, the kernels must be cooked for a long time, up to 24 hours. It also produces a bad smell while it is being cooked. Farmers say that excessive consumption of this plant causes stomachaches and intestinal problems. On the other hand, certain wild foods, which are collected and eaten even in times of food abundance, may become very important sources of famine-foods during times of food shortage. Some famine-foods are used as livestock fodder during normal times, but are consumed by humans only during severe food shortages.

Wild plants are often considered a low-status food, and people regard eating them as a source of shame. Usually, only children and poor families will eat these plants during non-famine times. Children are the most common harvesters and eaters of wild foods. Women also frequently gather wild food when they are on their way to collect firewood, fetch water, go to the market, or when they walk home from the fields.

Most Ethiopians, of course, generally neglect wild plants and eat only those that are commonly cultivated. Certain wild plants, such as the seed-producing *Amaranthus*, could have been fully domesticated and cultivated like any other food crop. Traditions, beliefs, and religious taboos, however, still block many people's willingness to domesticate and cultivate wild food plants. In the southern parts of Ethiopia, where there are still many tribes living with their native traditions and beliefs, there are fewer religious and other constraints than in other parts of the country. The daily diet of most people in southern Ethiopia includes a generous helping of wild foods, both plants and animals, during certain periods of the year.

The Ethiopian national dish is *injera*—a flat, circular pancake made of fermented dough. On top of this dough is placed a variety of cooked meats, vegetables, and pulses, such as beans and peas. Sauces are generally flavored with *berbere*, a blend of herbs and spices that includes hot peppers. Devout Ethiopian Orthodox Christians fast roughly half of the year and do not eat any meat or animal products. During these times, they enjoy a wide variety of salads, vegetables, and pulses.

WILDLIFE

Ethiopia's environmental diversity—ranging from scorching deserts and acacia savannas, to wetlands, woodlands, and cold alpine highlands—creates a great variety of natural habitats (places in which plants or animals can survive). Few countries in the world—and certainly few of Ethiopia's

This woman is cooking *injera*, the national dish of Ethiopia. It consists of a flat pancake to which meats, vegetables, and other ingredients are added.

size—contain a greater number of habitats. This, in turn, makes it possible for the country to have a wealth of wildlife.

The country is famous for its birds. Bird-watchers come from all over the world in the hope of seeing many of Ethiopia's estimated 800 bird species. In fact, about 20 of the species are endemic, meaning they can be found nowhere else in the world. The wattled ibis, the Abyssinian long claw, and the black-headed siskin are only a few of the many species of birds that can be observed both in and out of Ethiopia's national parks.

At one time, Ethiopia could also boast of having perhaps the greatest variety and abundance of wildlife in Africa. Sadly, this is no longer true today. Damage to habitat, over-hunting, and the introduction of livestock have combined to sharply reduce the country's once-rich wildlife resources. To an impoverished rural population, there is no distinction between a dwindling wildlife resource—such as a deer, antelope, or hartebeest—and meat to feed a hungry family. The country has created several national parks in an attempt to preserve its wildlife, as well as to encourage tourism. Tourism, after all, can and should be one of Ethiopia's chief sources of income. When most travelers think of Africa, they think of the continent's wonderful array of animals. Today, however, a traveler to Ethiopia searching for animal life would be sadly disappointed.

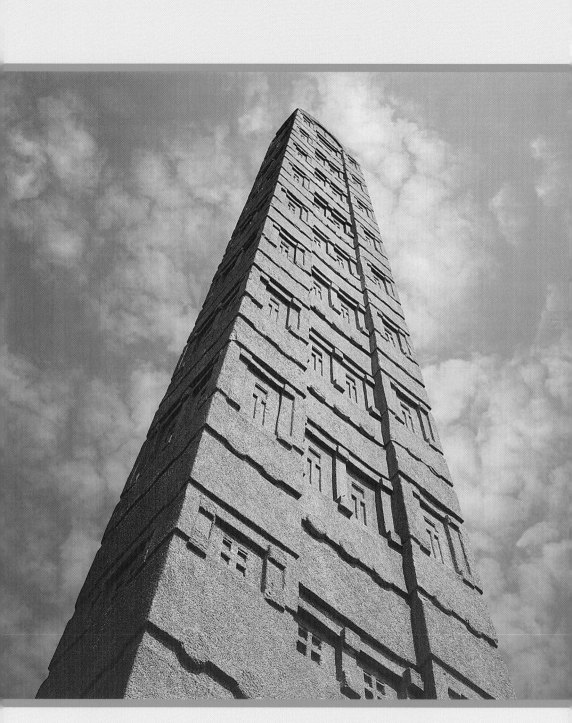

The ancient people of the kingdom of Aksum built and carved gigantic columns of stone to honor their deceased rulers.

3

Early History

Human history may have begun in or around what is now Ethiopia. Evidence of a pre-human presence dates back several million years. Traces of the earliest humans also have been found in the region. More recently, from the dawn of the historic period (time during which people have left tangible records), diverse peoples have inhabited the region in and around the Ethiopian highlands. For several thousand years, these groups united to produce a culture that differed greatly from the ways of life practiced by surrounding people. Many factors influenced the creation of this unique and distinctive culture.

ORIGINS OF HUMANITY

Many archaeologists believe that humanity originated in or near Ethiopia. East Africa's Great Rift Valley has yielded many pre-human and human skeletal remains that suggest that the area is the site of humankind's origins. In 1974, archaeologists excavating sites in the Awash River Valley of Ethiopia discovered 3.5 million-year-old fossils, which they named *Australopithecus afarensis.*

The more recent prehistoric populations of Ethiopia, those inhabiting the area several thousand years ago, spoke languages that belonged to the Afro-Asiatic language family. They included the Omotic, Cushitic, and Semitic languages, all of which are spoken in Ethiopia today. These early peoples hunted and gathered for thousands of years before they began to herd livestock. Several thousand years before the dawn of the Christian era, farming was established in the drier, grassier parts of the northern highlands. Native grasses such as *teff* (which is the main ingredient of the famous Ethiopian dish, *injera*) and *eleusine* were the first domesticated plants of Ethiopia. Barley and wheat were introduced much later from southwest Asia. Somewhat later, people began keeping domesticated animals—cattle, sheep, goats, and donkeys—which were also introduced from southwest Asia. Thus, from the late prehistoric period, the agricultural lifestyles that would be characteristic of Ethiopia through modern times were established.

It was the descendants of these early farmers who, at various times and places, interacted with successive waves of immigrants from across the Red Sea. During the first millennium B.C., and possibly even earlier, various groups from southwest Arabia began to cross the Red Sea and settle along the African coast and in the nearby highlands. These migrants brought with them their Semitic speech and script and their monumental stone architecture. The newcomers mixed with native Ethiopians to produce a culture known as pre-Aksumite. Trade probably played a large role in the settlement of this area. Archaeological evidence indicates that by the beginning of the Christian era, this culture had developed eastern and western variants. It was from the western branch, in the region of Aksum, that the powerful state of Aksum emerged.

AKSUM—ANCIENT KINGDOM AND TRADING STATE

The Aksumite Empire rose during the first century B.C. and flourished for perhaps a thousand years. It was one of Africa's most powerful and important early kingdoms. Aksum enjoyed its greatest power between the fourth and sixth centuries. By the eighth century, it had begun a gradual decline that lasted some four centuries. The heart of Aksum was in the highlands of what is today northern Ethiopia and part of neighboring Eritrea. Its major urban centers were at Aksum, a city in northern Ethiopia, and Adulis, a Red Sea port. Earlier centers, such as Yeha, also continued to flourish. At the kingdom's height, it extended along the Red Sea from Sawakin in present-day Sudan in the north to Berbera in present-day Somalia in the south. Aksum also reached as far inland as the Nile Valley in modern Sudan.

The growth of imperial traditions continued as the empire's foreign holdings expanded. This was especially true in southwest Arabia in the late second century A.D., and later in areas west of the Ethiopian highlands, including the kingdom of Meroe. Meroe was centered on the Nile River, north of the confluence (juncture) of the White Nile and Blue Nile. Its people were black Africans who were heavily influenced by Egyptian culture. It was probably the people of Meroe who were the first to be called *Aithiopiai*, or "burnt faces," by the Greeks. This term later gave rise to the name "Ethiopians," which was used in reference to the region including the northern highlands of the Horn of Africa and its inhabitants.

Sometime around A.D. 300, Aksumite armies conquered Meroe. By the early fourth century A.D., Aksumite King Ezana controlled a domain extending from southwest Arabia, west across the Red Sea to Meroe, and south from Sawakin to the southern coast of the Gulf of Aden. Ezana, like other Aksumite rulers, held the title *negusa nagast*, or "King of Kings." The title referred to his rule over numerous tribute-paying principalities. Ethiopian rulers continued to use this title into the mid-twentieth century.

The Aksumites developed a very high level of culture for their time. They created their own unique style of architecture and used it to build stone palaces and other public structures. They also built huge carved stone columns, called *stelae*, at Aksum. These monuments to deceased rulers are among the largest known stelae from the ancient world.

The Aksumites also had a written language. Of the early African kingdoms, only they and the people of Egypt and Meroe left written records of their civilization. These records were written in both Greek and Gi'iz (the ancestor of the modern Amharic and Tigrinya languages spoken in Ethiopia today). Greek was the language of trade in the eastern Mediterranean world of the day. Gi'iz is still used in Ethiopian Orthodox church services.

Aksumites also minted coins for more than 300 years. This practice was totally unique in ancient Africa. Many of the coins were inlaid with gold, silver, or bronze, and the images and dates provide a chronology of Aksum's rulers. Establishment of the Christian church was one Aksum's most important contributions to Ethiopian tradition. Around A.D. 330–340, King Ezana converted to Christianity, and made it the official state religion of Aksum, after which it spread rapidly throughout the region.

Little is known about fifth-century Aksum. Early in the sixth century, however, Aksumite rulers reasserted their control over southwest Arabia, though only for a short time. Later in the sixth century, Persians established a toehold in Yemen and ended Aksumite control there. The Persians also attacked Egypt and further disrupted the Aksumite trade networks in the Red Sea area. Over the next century and a half, Aksum was increasingly cut off from its overseas trading ports. This resulted in the beginning of a four-century period of gradual decline. As it lost influence elsewhere, Aksum began to withdraw into the highland interior of northern Ethiopia.

THE EARLY ISLAMIC PERIOD

During the seventh and eighth centuries, the Islamic religion spread like wildfire from its place of origin on the Arabian Peninsula. Its spread had a great impact on Aksum. By the time the prophet Muhammad died in A.D. 632, the entire Arabian Peninsula and all the lands surrounding the Red Sea had come under the influence of this new faith. Although Islam often spread by conquest, its relations with Aksum were not hostile at first. An Islamic tradition holds that before Muhammad rose to power, there was much trouble in Arabia. During this period of conflict, some members of Muhammad's family and some of his early converts took refuge with the Aksumites. Because of their help, Aksum was spared the *jihad*, or holy war, that accompanied much of the spread of Islam. Muhammad himself supposedly warned his followers never to harm Ethiopians.

The Arabs considered Aksum to be of the same level of importance as the Islamic state, the Byzantine Empire, and China—the world's greatest kingdoms at that time. However, problems soon developed between Aksum and the new Islamic power. Egypt and other areas in the eastern Mediterranean region had become Muslim. This greatly reduced Aksum's relations with the Byzantine Empire, another major Christian power. The spread of Muslim beliefs isolated the Christians in Aksum.

Perhaps of even greater importance, Islamic expansion threatened Aksum's maritime contacts. They were already under siege by Persians. Now, they faced a challenge from

Muslim fleets that controlled the Red Sea. By the mid-seventh century, Aksum began to lose its maritime trade routes. By the mid-ninth century, Arab traders had moved southward and gained a foothold on the coast of east Africa. Soon, most people in eastern Africa had become Muslims. East of Ethiopia's central highlands, Ifat, a Muslim sultanate, was formed at the dawn of the twelfth century. Many surrounding peoples were gradually converted to Islam. The Christians in Ethiopia's northern highlands region began to feel as though Aksum were an isolated island, surrounded by a sea of Muslims.

THE ZAGWE DYNASTY

The Aksumite people had lost their maritime commercial network. They also were suffering at the hands of an expanding Islamic empire. Because of these hardships, the Aksumites began to turn their attention to colonizing the Ethiopian highlands. The old capital at Aksum had been abandoned by the mid-seventh century. The community was left to become a religious center. The culture of Aksum spread slowly south-ward over the next several centuries. Military colonies were established. They, in turn, served as population centers from which Aksumite culture—including the Semitic language and Christianity—spread to the surrounding population. By the tenth century, a post-Aksumite Christian kingdom had emerged. It controlled an area that included Ethiopia's central northern highlands from modern Eritrea to Shewa, and the Red Sea coast from old Adulis to Zeila in present-day Somalia.

By 1137, a new dynasty had emerged in Ethiopia's high-land Christian stronghold. It was known as the Zagwe. This dynasty lasted for a period of almost 150 years, under the rule of 11 different kings. The Zagwe grew out of the long political and cultural contact between Cushitic- and Semitic-speaking peoples in the northern highlands. The

During the Zagwe dynasty, which created a major center for the Christian religion, the people of Ethiopia built many beautiful churches. Some of them were carved of rock, like this one in Lalibela.

Zagwe were devout Christians who believed that they were commanded by God to build a replica of Jerusalem in Africa. As a result, they built many new churches and monasteries. Eleven great churches, all in the shape of crosses, were carved into volcanic rock around the capital at Adefa. In time, Adefa became known as Lalibela, named for the Zagwe king believed to have been responsible for building the Adefa churches.

By the time of the Zagwe, the Ethiopian church was showing the effects of long centuries of isolation from the rest of the Christian world. Since Egypt's conquest by Muslim Arabs in the seventh century, the Ethiopians limited contact was with the Egyptian Coptic Christian church, which supplied the Ethiopian church with a patriarch, or *abun*, upon royal request. From the seventh to the twelfth century, the Ethiopian Orthodox Church began to place a very strong emphasis on Old Testament beliefs and practices. This emphasis separated it from the European Christian Church and even from the Coptic Christian Church of Egypt.

During the Zagwe dynasty, Ethiopian Christians maintained regular contact with the Egyptians. The Ethiopian church had demonstrated that it was not seeking new converts. Rather, it focused its attention on areas of the highlands where people were already followers of Christianity. Not until the fourteenth and fifteenth centuries did the church once again demonstrate a strong interest in converting nonbelievers.

RESTORATION OF THE "SOLOMONIC" LINE

The Amhara were an increasingly powerful people who took their name from their region, Amhara, which was located south of the Zagwe. In the year 1270, an Amhara noble, Yekuno Amlak, drove out the last Zagwe ruler and proclaimed himself king. His rise to power was another step southward for the Christian kingdom of Ethiopia. The new dynasty that Yekuno Amlak founded came to be known as the "Solomonic" dynasty. The title referred to the fact that the kings claimed to be descended from King Solomon of ancient Israel.

According to tradition, the line of Aksum kings originated with the offspring of a union between King Solomon and the Queen of Sheba. Because of this, the idea arose that royal legitimacy came from descent in a line of Solomonic kings. The Tigray and Amhara peoples denied the Zagwe any share in this heritage; they believed the Zagwe had gained power by force. When Yekuno Amlak took the throne, he was looked upon as a legitimate return of the Solomonic line. All Ethiopian kings since his time have traced their legitimacy to him, and thereby, to Solomon and the Queen of Sheba.

Amhara became the geographical and political center of the Christian kingdom under Yekuno Amlak. The king concentrated on consolidating his power and control over the northern highlands. At the same time, he focused on trying to weaken and destroy the encircling "pagan" and Muslim states. He enjoyed great success against the Islamic sultanate of Ifat, located to the southeast of Amhara.

When Yekuno Amlak died in 1285, his son, Yagba Seyon, took over, and reigned until 1294. However, there were many power struggles among his descendants during the period following his reign. Because of this family fighting, a new rule was introduced in 1300. It stated that all males tracing descent from Yekuno Amlak (except the reigning emperor and his sons) were to be held in a mountaintop prison. This prison was almost impossible to reach and it was closely guarded by soldiers who were loyal to the king. Most kings followed this practice until the early sixteenth century, when the prison was destroyed. The royal prison helped solve a problem that plagued the Solomonic line through its long history—constant fighting over succession among those claiming royal lineage.

AMHARA DYNASTY

Yekuno Amlak's grandson, Amda Siyon, distinguished himself by at last establishing firm control over all of the Christian districts of Ethiopia. He even expanded his kingdom into the neighboring regions of Shewa, Gojan, and Damot, and to Agew districts near Lake Tana. He spent a great deal of time and effort battling the Muslim states to the east and southeast of Amhara. These districts, like Ifat, posed a powerful threat to his kingdom. His victories gave him control over the central highlands and strengthened his influence over the trade routes to the Red Sea. His conquests also helped spread Christianity in the southern highlands.

In 1436, Zara Yakob was crowned king, a position he held until 1468. He proved to be one of Ethiopia's greatest rulers. In 1445, his armies scored a dramatic victory over the sultanate of Adal and its Muslim allies. For two centuries, these tribes had been a source of determined opposition to the Christians of the Ethiopian highlands.

Some of Zara Yakob's most notable achievements were in religious matters. He sponsored a reorganization of the Christian Orthodox Church and tried to unify its religious practices. He also encouraged the spread of Christianity among nonbelievers.

Because the Islamic challenge was always a threat, Zara Yakob continued to mold Christianity into Ethiopia's main line of internal defense. He fought Muslim control of shipping around the Horn of Africa. Reports of his success made their way to Europe, which added to the mystique of the legendary Christian king, Prester John, who many west Europeans believed ruled a land someplace in southwestern Asia or northeastern Asia. Some European leaders exaggerated the importance of Ethiopia, hoping to reduce Muslim influence in Egypt, Arabia, and Syria.

Zara Yakob was a very strong ruler. His successors were weak, however, which caused the Solomonic monarchy to decline.

Beginning in the fourteenth century, the power of the negusa nagast, or "King of kings," as the emperor was called, was nearly unlimited, at least in theory. In practice, though, his power often was rather limited. The kingdom's unity depended upon the emperor 's ability to control the governors of the various realms. Governors had their own local bases of support. As long as they paid their royal tribute and rounded up men for the emperor's military campaigns, they were left alone and could function fairly independently. When the military had to be used, it was supported by local taxes and lived off the land. The result was that the emperor paid very little for their services, leaving the provinces to contribute the lion's share to the campaigns. Failure to honor obligations to the throne could bring the wrath of the emperor's forces, and possible plunder of the district and removal of the local governor.

The emperor lived in seclusion. He was even shielded, except on rare occasions, from the gaze of all but his personal servants and high court officials. Most other subjects were forbidden access to the emperor. Great protocol and ceremony enhanced his status as a descendant of King Solomon and the Queen of Sheba.

DECLINE OF THE CHRISTIAN KINGDOM AND THE RISE OF ISLAMIC STATES

By the thirteenth century, the Christian kingdom of Ethiopia, then ruled by the Amhara, was threatened by Muslim encirclement. By that time, various peoples east and south of the highlands had converted to Islam. Some of these groups had established powerful sultanates. Two of the most powerful were the sultanate of Ifat, in the northeastern foothills, and the sultanate established in the Islamic city of Harer farther east. Two other important groups of people also lived along the Red Sea coast—the Afar and the Somali.

For the most part, Islamic people inhabited small, independent states. Often, they were divided by differences in culture, including language. Many of them spoke Cushitic languages, unlike the Semitic speakers of Harer. Some were farmers and traders; others herded flocks of sheep, goats, and cattle. These differences made it difficult for them to unify.

Even though they were not unified, the Muslim states continued to pose a threat to the Christian kingdom. By the late fourteenth century, descendants of the ruling family of Ifat had moved east to the area around Harer. They reestablished the old Muslim sultanate of Adal, which had become the most powerful Muslim stronghold in the Horn of Africa. It controlled the important trading routes from the Ethiopian highlands to the port of Zeila. This posed a grave threat to Ethiopia's commerce and to Christian control of the highlands.

From the mid-fifteenth through the mid-seventeenth century, aggressive Muslim states confronted the Christian Ethiopians. At the same time, the Portuguese also tried to convert the Ethiopians to Roman Catholicism, which caused a great deal of conflict. By the mid-seventeenth century, the kingdom of Ethiopia had greatly weakened. As a result, regional leaders became independent of the emperor's rule.

The Christian state had been unable to gain control over the Muslim states to the east. Still, it had successfully resisted Muslim incursions through the fourteenth and most of the fifteenth centuries. As the long reign of Zara Yakob came to an end, however, the kingdom of Ethiopia once again experienced problems of succession. The emperor always had several wives, and each wife actively pushed for her own sons to become the next emperor. One or more generations of dynastic conflict seriously weakened a kingdom that had been held together by a strong warrior king. To make matters worse, frequent raids and counterraids between the

Christian and Muslim powers intensified and continued into the sixteenth century. Each side tried to capture as many slaves and as much booty (treasure) as possible.

By the mid-sixteenth century, a young Muslim soldier named Ahmed ibn Ibraham al Ghazi won a large following thanks to his military prowess. In time, he became the leader of Adal. Al Ghazi was also a religious leader. He rallied the ethnically diverse Muslims in a jihad intended to end Christian power in the region. In 1525, al Ghazi led his first expedition against a Christian army. Over the next two or three years, he continued to attack Ethiopian territory, burning churches, taking prisoners, and collecting booty. At the Battle of Shimbra Kure in 1525, al Ghazi broke the Christian backbone of resistance. The Ethiopian emperor at the time, Lebna Dengel, was unable to defend his kingdom against the onslaught. In 1528, al Ghazi defeated the Christian forces and penetrated the very heartland of Ethiopia. After devastating the countryside, he put much of the Christian kingdom under Muslim rule.

By 1535, al Ghazi's kingdom spread from the Ethiopian highlands to the Red Sea. In that same year, Ethiopia turned to Europe for help. Portugal responded with several hundred soldiers. In 1543, the Ethiopians joined forces with a small group of Portuguese soldiers to defeat the Muslim army. In the battle, al Ghazi was killed. The death of their powerful leader destroyed the unity of the Muslim forces. Christian armies slowly pushed them back until the highlands of Ethiopia were once again under Christian control.

Despite this victory, Ethiopians had suffered terrible losses during the struggle against al Ghazi. Herds of live-stock had been slaughtered, communities destroyed, and many people captured and sold into slavery by the Muslims. It took centuries for the Ethiopians to recover fully. Even today, the bitter war remains a vivid memory to many Ethiopians.

OROMO MIGRATIONS

In the mid-sixteenth century, the Christian kingdom began to feel pressure from the Oromo people who lived to the south and southeast. The Oromo began migrating into southern Ethiopia. They were a pastoral people who liked to fight. This love of warfare, combined with an expanding population of both people and cattle, caused the Oromo to move into neighboring territory. They were not interested in establishing an empire or imposing a religion, as the highland Christians and the lowland Muslims were. They simply wanted new land and pastures for their livestock.

During the second half of the sixteenth century, the Oromo descended on the Ethiopian highlands. Their migration came in waves, and lacked any semblance of unity. They fought among each other as much as they fought with their new neighbors. As they moved farther from their homeland, many Oromo changed their ways, joining with the Amhara and becoming Christians. No matter how much they changed, though, Oromo groups retained their language and sense of local identity.

The Oromo migration caused a weakening of both Christian and Muslim power and drove a wedge between the two faiths along the eastern edge of the highlands. The Ethiopian state was fragmented and left much smaller, with a large group of strangers in its midst. The Oromo continued to play a major part in the history of Ethiopia as they assimilated and slowly became part of the Christian kingdom.

CONTACT WITH EUROPE

During the fourteenth and fifteenth centuries, Egyptian Muslims had destroyed the neighboring Christian states in the Nile valley. For centuries after the Muslim conquests, Ethiopia's only connection with the larger Christian world was through Egypt's Coptic Church.

Occasionally, Ethiopian pilgrims would travel to the Holy Land. Ethiopian monks from Jerusalem attended the Council of Florence in 1441 at the Pope's invitation. The Pope wanted to reunite the Eastern and Western churches. Westerners learned about Ethiopia through the monks and pilgrims, and they became attracted to it for two main reasons. First, many believed Ethiopia was the long-sought land of the legendary Christian priest-king of the East, Prester John. Second, the West viewed Ethiopia as a potentially valuable ally in the struggle against the Islamic forces that continued to threaten southern Europe.

Portugal expressed interest in this potential ally by sending a representative to Ethiopia in 1493. The Ethiopians, in turn, sent an envoy to Portugal in 1509 to request a coordinated attack against the Muslims. Although the Portuguese had assisted the Christian Ethiopians earlier in defeating and killing al Ghazi, they still insisted on trying to convert the Ethiopians to Roman Catholicism. Portuguese Roman Catholic missionaries arrived in the 1554. At least two Ethiopian emperors reportedly converted to Roman Catholicism. After the second Roman Catholic emperor abdicated in favor of his son, all Jesuits (an order of priests in the Catholic Church) were expelled from Ethiopia, and other Roman Catholic missionaries soon followed. The intense conflict over conversions left Ethiopians with a feeling of deep hostility toward foreign Christians and Europeans that continued into the twentieth century and contributed to Ethiopia's isolation from Europe for 200 years.

GONDER STATE

From 1632 to 1667, Ethiopia was ruled by Emperor Fasiladas. During his reign, he kept out the disruptive Catholic Christians, dealt with sporadic Muslim incursions, and tried to reestablish central authority. He resumed the practice of confining royal family members in a remote mountaintop prison, and reconstructed a cathedral at Aksum that had been destroyed by al Ghazi. Fasiladas established his camp at Gonder. The site became the permanent capital, as well as the cultural and political center of Ethiopia, during the Gonder period. Several impressive churches also were constructed there. One of the most famous and beautiful churches was the Debre Birthan Selassie.

The Gonder period saw a flowering of art and architecture that lasted more than a century. However, Gonder emperors never regained the full control they once had over wealth and labor. Many nobles became virtually independent of central authority. The Gonder kings were reduced to mere ceremonial figureheads, while the military functions and real power lay with the powerful nobles. The kingdom of Ethiopia did not officially exist during this time period. Instead, the various districts were ruled by independent nobles who warred constantly among themselves.

At the beginning of the nineteenth century, Ethiopia was a Gonder state that consisted of the northern and central highlands and the immediately adjacent lowlands. The state was a monarchy in name only, as the nobles fought for the military title of *ras*, or marshal. The highest title was that of *rasbitwoded*, which combined supreme military command with the duties of first minister at court. These nobles had the ability to enthrone or depose lesser nobles at will.

The major ethnic groups making up the state at this time were the Amhara and the Tigray peoples, who spoke Semitic, and the Oromo. In terms of numbers, the Oromo were dominant. They were Cushitic speakers, but were neither politically nor culturally unified. Many Oromo had converted to Christianity by the early 1800s. Very often, their conversion was accompanied by assimilation into the Amhara or Tigray culture. At the edges of the highlands, many people had converted to Islam, especially in the areas of the former sultanates of Ifat and Adal. The Oromo people, whether

Christian or Amhara in culture, played important political roles in the *Zemene Mesafint*, or "Era of the Princes," as this period of time is often called. Sometimes the Oromo people helped aspiring Amharans gain positions of power, and other times, they became kingmakers and *rases* in their own right. In the southern region, some Oromo groups started kingdoms of their own.

The seventeenth through the nineteenth century was a period of migration and cultural integration. Various groups freely borrowed techniques and institutions from each other. In the south, Islam made substantial inroads. Oromo chieftains found Islam a handy tool in building trade networks and centralizing their territories.

By the middle of the nineteenth century, Europeans, especially the British and French, showed great interest in the Horn of Africa. Egypt made incursions along the Ethiopian coast and tried to gain control of the Red Sea ports. Competition for trade combined with differences in opinion about how to respond to Egypt's activities were important factors in the conflicts of the period.

At this time, another major figure emerged in Gonder— Kasa Haylu—the son of a lesser noble from a district on the border shared with Sudan. Kasa was a soldier of fortune who eventually impressed those in power in Gonder. They awarded him with the governorship of a minor province. He also married the daughter of Ras Ali, a Christian of Oromo background who dominated the court at Gonder. Kasa rebelled against Ali and occupied Gonder in 1847. He forced Ali to recognize him as chief of the western frontier area. Kasa eventually defeated Ali's army and burned Ali's capital at Debre Tabor. In 1854, Kasa assumed the title *negus*, or "king," and in 1855, the head of the Ethiopian Orthodox Church crowned him Tewodros II.

Tewodros II tried very hard to reestablish a cohesive Ethiopian state and to reform its administration and church.

One of his first tasks was to bring the province of Shewa under his control. In the course of subduing the Shewans, Tewodros imprisoned a prince, Menelik, who would later become emperor himself. Constant rebellion in the other provinces kept Tewodros very busy over the next several years. The drain on Tewodros's resources, energy, and manpower limited his ability to deal with other issues that needed attention. By 1865, Menelik had escaped from prison and joined with many other new rebels in Tewodros's kingdom.

In addition to his conflicts with rebels and rivals, Tewodros had problems with European powers. He asked the British government for aid, but then took the British representatives hostage because he was unhappy with the response. In 1868, a British force from India set out for Ethiopia to gain release of the hostages. As the British stormed his stronghold, Tewodros committed suicide.

Tewodros II never realized his goal of restoring a strong monarchy to Ethiopia. He did take some very important steps, however. He established the rule that governors and judges must be salaried appointees. He also established a professional army, so he would not have to depend on local lords to provide soldiers. Tewodros also tried to reform the church. He thought members of the clergy were ignorant and immoral. After failing in an attempt to tax church lands to help fund government activities, he confiscated the land. This act made him many enemies in the church. Tewodros II was an excellent military strategist, but a very poor politician.

REIGN OF MENELIK II

Emperor Tewodros II died in 1868. At that time, Menelik, a ruler of Shoa in central Ethiopia, was gaining strength. With Italian support, he was able to seize the throne after the death of Emperor Johannes IV in 1889. Menelik successfully extended his empire. At the same time, though, European

King Menelik II (center), who lived from 1844 to 1913, took over the throne of Ethiopia in 1889, with Italy's help. During his reign, Menelik tried to modernize the country and to use his dealings with the strong nations of Europe to bring Ethiopia advantages.

colonial powers were showing an interest in the territories surrounding Ethiopia. Menelik considered the Italians a major challenge and negotiated a treaty with them in 1889. The treaty permitted the Italians to establish a toehold on the edge of the northern highlands. From there, they sought to expand into Tigray (in northern Ethiopia). Relations were tense at best. Finally, Menelik repaid a loan to the Italian government that freed him from the treaty.

Eritrea, meanwhile, became an Italian colony, and the

Italians were exploring Somalia as well. Great Britain encouraged the Italians to keep their influence over Ethiopia in order to stabilize the region. France, however, encouraged the Ethiopians to oppose the Italian threat by clearly establishing the political boundaries of their empire. France reduced the size of its territorial claims in French Somaliland, and recognized Ethiopian sovereignty in the area. Menelik wisely cooperated with both the French and the British in putting down rebellions in the neighboring territories of Sudan and Somaliland. He was skillful at playing one foreign colonial power off another, thereby avoiding having to make any major concessions.

Menelik died in 1913. He had taken many important steps to strengthen and modernize his domain. He had established his capital in Addis Ababa, a community in southern Shewa. This led to the rise of a genuine urban center in the country. He had also hired a French company to build a railroad linking Addis Ababa and Djibouti, which was completed in 1917. During his rule, Menelik also attempted to end the slave trade and stop the long practice of feudal nobility. His conquests doubled the size of the country and brought present-day southern Ethiopia, with its large Muslim population, into the realm.

RAS TAFARI ERA

After Menelik died, fear of civil war prompted the court to keep his death secret for some time. For a number of years, there was a constant struggle for power. Finally, in 1930, 17 years after Menelik's death, Ras Tafari succeeded to the throne without contest, taking the name Haile Selassie I.

Tafari began to modernize Ethiopia. He obtained administrative regulations and legal codebooks from various European countries and used them to find models he could adopt for his own government. Tafari also supported government schooling in the belief that Ethiopia needed well-educated men if it hoped to develop and be well governed. He also took steps to improve health care and social services.

Earlier, in 1919, as regent, Tafari tried to gain membership for Ethiopia in the League of Nations, but was refused because of the existence of slavery in the country. He banned the slave trade in 1923, and Ethiopia was then unanimously elected to the League. In 1924, Ethiopia passed laws that gradually freed all slaves and their children. Slavery had long been practiced in Ethiopia, as well as in a number of other African countries. Most slaves worked in households, where they were considered second-class members of the family. In 1928, Ethiopia signed a friendship treaty with Italy that provided for an Ethiopian free-trade zone at Aseb in Eritrea. In 1930, negotiations began with various international banking institutions for the establishment of the Bank of Ethiopia. The country was on the brink of entering the modern era.

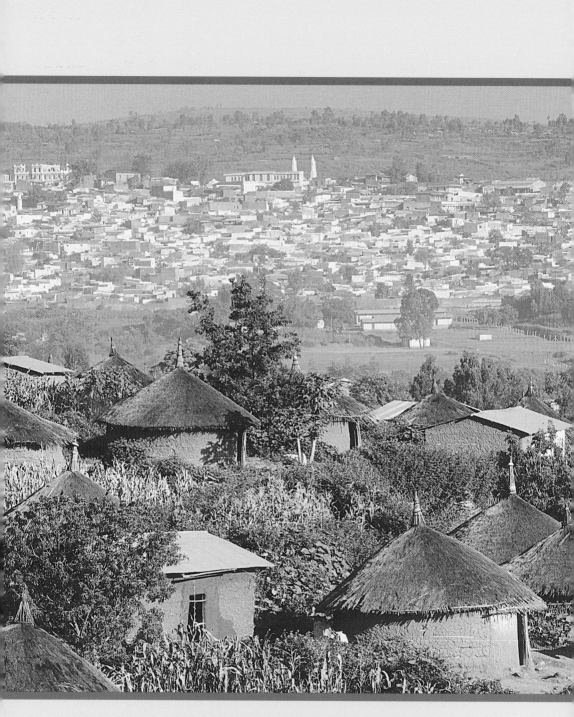

The sharp contrast between Ethiopia's developing cities and the lifestyles of rural people can be seen in this photograph of Harer, in which the large city forms a backdrop for a cluster of traditional huts.

4

Recent History

Ethiopia's recent history has been turbulent. The country has marvelous environmental diversity, holds a vast store of natural resources, and has a population of more than 60 million people. Yet it has not been able to realize its great potential for several reasons.

HAILE SELASSIE AND RASTAFARIANISM

How does one explain why a thousand or so people from the Caribbean island of Jamaica might live in Ethiopia? Part of the answer lies in one the most important events in twentieth-century Ethiopian history. In April 1930, Ras Tafari was crowned Haile Selassie I, assuming the title "Conquering Lion of the Tribe of Judah, Elect of God, and King of Kings of Ethiopia." Many black leaders in the United States and the Caribbean believed that Ras Tafari fulfilled a biblical prophecy that black kings would come out of Africa someday. He was judged by many to be more than a ruler; some thought he was God returning to Earth. It was this belief that led to the beginning of the Rastafarian movement.

Rastafarianism is a combined religious and cultural movement. It began in Jamaica in 1930 with the crowning of Haile Selassie. The religious aspect of the movement is based on the belief that Ras Tafari is the Messiah, or savior. Socially, believers tend to reject European culture, including its ideas and values, and are particularly noted for their use of *ganja*, or marijuana. Reggae music has played a major role in the spread of Rastafarian beliefs. One of the primary means of spreading "Rasta" themes, in fact, was the music of Jamaican reggae singers, particularly the late Bob Marley. Today, there are an estimated 180,000 Rastafarians worldwide.

In response to the growing movement, a small number of Rastafarian Jamaicans migrated to Ethiopia. Haile Selassie encouraged this back-to-Africa movement. In 1955, he gave 500 acres of his own land on which "black people of the West" were encouraged to settle. Several thousand Jamaicans accepted his offer and moved to Shashemmene, a market town of about 50,000 people located some 170 miles south of Addis Ababa. At the peak of settlement, about 2,500 Jamaicans had relocated, many of them farmers. Today, only about 1,000 of them remain in Ethiopia.

Haile Selassie ruled as emperor for 45 years. He was Ethiopia's last imperial leader. During his rule, he made many reforms aimed at modernizing Ethiopia and breaking the authority of the small number of wealthy and powerful nobles. Rules were passed that forced *rases* either to obey the emperor or be found guilty of treason against him. A new constitution adopted when he came to power in 1930 guaranteed the powerful status of the emperor. It ensured that when Haile Selassie was no longer able to rule, power would remain with his line of successors. The emperor

Haile Selassie ruled as Ethiopia's emperor for 45 years. Although he kept most political power in his own hands, he also created a new constitution and worked to provide better services for the people. Still, many Ethiopians were dissatisfied with his reign.

retained all control over central and local government, including the judiciary, the legislature, and the military. The constitution was really an effort to provide a legal basis for replacing provincial rulers with appointees who were loyal to the emperor.

Selassie took many nonmilitary measures to promote loyalty to the throne and to the state. He established new elementary and secondary schools in Addis Ababa, and sent some 150 university-age students abroad to study. Ethiopia enacted a fair penal code. It also imported printing presses to provide nationally oriented newspapers. The availability of electricity and telephone services was increased, as were various public health measures. The Bank of Ethiopia, founded in 1931, began to issue Ethiopian currency.

ITALIAN RULE AND WORLD WAR II

Italy was a latecomer to the European scramble for African colonies. It first became established in Eritrea in the 1880s. Here, a succession of Italian governors success-fully maintained a degree of unity and public order in a region marked by great cultural diversity. In the late 1920s, Italy affirmed its treaty of friendship with Ethiopia. Even so, it soon became clear that Italy wanted to expand its holdings and that Ethiopia was in its sights. In order to provoke an excuse for war, Italy deliberately began to antagonize Ethiopia.

On October 3, 1935, Italy attacked Ethiopia from Eritrea without a declaration of war. The League of Nations imme-diately declared Italy the aggressor, but took no further action. During the seven-month conflict, Ethiopian forces were no match for the more powerful Italian forces. Ethiopia's forces put up a valiant defense, but were unable to compete against the Italians, who had superior air power and even used chemical weapons. Fearing for his life, Haile Selassie fled to French Somaliland on May 2, 1936, and became an emperor in exile. With Ethiopia's long tradition of strong warrior emperors, this was not something to which the people were accustomed.

Italian forces took Addis Ababa on May 5, and four days later, Italy claimed control of Ethiopia. One month later,

Haile Selassie made a moving speech before the League of Nations. In it, he said the member nations had two choices: support for collective security or international lawlessness. His speech was so powerful and well received that he became a major international figure. The United States and Soviet Union refused to recognize Italy's control of Ethiopia, although France and Great Britain did. Italy soon united Ethiopia, Eritrea, and Italian Somaliland into one single administrative unit divided into six provinces. Strong Ethiopian resistance continued, however.

After a failed assassination attempt on an Italian leader, colonial authorities executed 30,000 Ethiopians, including nearly half of the younger, educated population. This harsh policy failed to settle the unrest, so in November 1937, a new Italian governor was appointed to Ethiopia. He undertook large-scale public works projects such as the construction of the country's first system of improved roads.

Meanwhile, Haile Selassie was still in exile, trying to gain support from Western countries. When Italy entered World War II on the side of Germany, Great Britain sought to cooperate with Ethiopia and to chase the Italians out of both Ethiopia and British Somaliland. On May 5, 1941, Haile Selassie reentered Addis Ababa with the help of British military forces. It was not until January 1942, however, that the last of the Italian troops surrendered to British and Ethiopian forces. Ethiopia and Great Britain reached an agreement in which the British would help organize and train a new Ethiopian army. The terms of the agreement confirmed Ethiopia's status as a sovereign state.

After Haile Selassie returned to the throne in 1941, the British assumed control over Ethiopia's currency and foreign exchange, as well as its imports and exports. The British also helped Ethiopia rebuild its government. These changes, plus the modernizations that had been brought about by the Italians, convinced Ethiopia that it needed to concentrate on modernization if it was to survive as an independent state.

THE POST WORLD WAR II PERIOD

After World War II, Ethiopians believed that everything would go back into place as it had been before the Italian takeover. They accepted the idea of monarchy and the privileges rulers held as leaders of both the government and the church. A desire for change, however, was stirring in the country. New social classes had emerged, and a younger and increasingly frustrated generation that was full of expectations clashed with older Ethiopians who insisted on maintaining traditional systems.

In March 1942, Haile Selassie announced a new tax system that divided all land into one of three categories: fertile, semifertile, and poor. A fixed tax was imposed for each 40-hectare (about 100 acres) parcel of land, depending on its category. The nobles refused to accept any change in the existing land tenure system and successfully fought the government over the issue. The emperor acknowledged defeat and settled for a flat 10 percent tithe (levy) on all but church lands. The problem was that this tax was simply passed on by the landlords to their tenants. Finally, in 1951, Haile Selassie further reduced the land tax payable by landlords. Still, the peasants continued to carry the entire taxation burden, as they had for centuries.

Haile Selassie also pressed for reforms in the Ethiopian Orthodox Church. In July 1948, he took steps by which he, rather than the patriarch of Alexandria, Egypt, would choose the *abun*, or patriarch of the Ethiopian Orthodox Church. For the first time in 16 centuries of Ethiopian Christianity, an Ethiopian rather than an Egyptian served as the head of the Ethiopian church. The postwar years also saw a change in the relationship between church and state. The clergy lost the right to try fellow church officials for civil offenses in a separate court. Vast church landholdings would also now be taxed.

Haile Selassie was very active on the diplomatic front. Ethiopia was a founding member of the United Nations (UN) and the Organization of African Unity (OAU). In 1953, the emperor asked the United States for military assistance and economic support. Although he grew increasingly dependent on the United States, he also asked various other countries for help, including the Soviet Union and China.

As a reformer, Haile Selassie realized that he had to compromise. He had to keep the support of the church and the nobility in order to keep Ethiopia strong and united. Political changes were few, and whenever Haile Selassie made a new law, he backed down if it met with any resistance. The emperor placed the local government in the hands of the central administration in Addis Ababa and revised the administrative divisions. By the mid-1960s, he had divided Ethiopia into 14 provinces. Each province was under a governor general appointed directly by the emperor. The provinces were further subdivided into smaller and smaller units. This political structure turned out to be inefficient because local power was held exclusively by high-ranking landed nobles. Younger, well-educated officials became frustrated. They were given low-ranking positions, and superiors treated their work with contempt.

The emperor created a national judiciary and appointed its judges. In 1955, he announced a revised constitution. It further proclaimed the religious origins of the emperor's power and continued the centralization process. Haile Selassie also hoped to gain the support of well-educated Ethiopians who earned their livelihood from modern economic activities. This new elite was the product of a small number of secondary schools run by foreign staffs. Although most of the students were from families of the landed nobility, they were strongly influenced by their democratically oriented Western teachers and by other students who came from less wealthy and powerful families.

In 1960, a coup was staged in Addis Ababa while Haile Selassie was out of the country. The rebels seized the crown prince and more than 20 cabinet ministers and other government leaders. The rebel leaders hoped to establish a government that would improve the social and economic conditions of all Ethiopians. They wanted to keep the traditional authority of the crown prince, but made no mention of the emperor. The Ethiopian people, however, did not support the coup's leaders. Even though university students demonstrated in favor of the coup, both the military and the church remained loyal to the emperor. The coup was a dismal failure, but it served to polarize traditional and modern forces in Ethiopia and to rob the emperor of his claim to universal acceptance.

BACKGROUND FOR REVOLUTION

Opposition to Haile Selassie mounted during the last 14 years of his reign. After the 1960 coup attempt, the emperor tried to reclaim loyalty by stepping up reform. He gave police officers and military officials land grants. No real changes occurred in economic or social development, however. In 1965, student demonstrations called for land reform and an end to corruption and rising prices. In the mid-1960s, a modern tax system was submitted to Parliament. All land had to be registered. The hope was that this would eventually strip the landed nobility of their wealth and power. Powerful landowners strongly opposed these proposals. The emperor faced stern opposition to change in every part of Ethiopia.

The government clearly had been unsuccessful in bringing about economic and political reforms since the 1960 coup attempt. This was a major factor in the revolution that began in 1974. Rising inflation, corruption, and a severe famine that affected several provinces were also factors that contributed to the growing unrest. Fearing another coup attempt, Selassie deliberately fostered division in the military in order to keep troops from uniting in a coup against him. He feared a time when any person or group might become powerful enough to unseat him from his throne.

The military was becoming more and more dissatisfied. Soldiers lived in substandard housing. The food, supplies, and pay they received were very inadequate. Many were unhappy with what they believed was a weak and slow government role in famine relief. The middle class was becoming increasingly upset over the lack of civil freedoms. Low teachers' salaries, increased fuel prices, and the need for land reform also contributed to the rising tide of unrest and the desire for a new political system.

DAWN OF A NEW ERA: THE *DERG*

Finally, in January 1974, an army branch of the military mutinied and Ethiopians rioted in the capital. Haile Selassie's grip on the country was weakening. In June, a small group of about 120 military men, none of whom was above the rank of major, organized themselves into a body called the Coordinating Committee of the Armed Forces, Police, and Territorial Army. The group elected Major Mengistu Haile Mariam as chairman. This anonymous group became known as the *Derg* (Amharic for "committee" or "council"). It was to become the leading force in Ethiopia's government, including its political and military affairs, for the next 13 years. During this period, no new members were added to the Derg. When a member was lost, he was not replaced. At first, the Derg remained behind the scenes. Later, however, the leaders emerged from anonymity to become the official governing personnel.

Although at first it did not officially control the government, the Derg held the real power. It could mobilize troops, for example, and challenge the emperor. Initially, the Derg claimed allegiance to the emperor. At the same time, though, it arrested members of the aristocracy, military, and government who continued to support Selassie. It was also successful in wringing some concessions from the emperor. Political prisoners were released, a new constitution was written, and exiles were allowed to return to Ethiopia.

By July 1974, Haile Selassie's power had greatly weakened as the Derg continued to expand its influence. By late August, the emperor had lost almost all his power. He also faced charges of deliberately covering up the vast famines that plagued the country throughout the early 1970s. Finally, in September 1974, Haile Selassie was arrested and the Derg seized power. Having been successful in deposing the emperor, the Derg renamed itself the Provisional Military Administrative Council (PMAC) and proclaimed itself Ethiopia's ruling body. In January 1975, it announced "Ethiopia First" as its guiding policy.

THE ROAD TO SOCIALISM

Lieutenant General Aman Mikael Andom was not a member of the Derg, but he had lent his good name to its efforts to reform the imperial regime. He was a well-known and popular commander, and a hero of the 1960s war against Somalia. Andom became head of state and chairman of the Council of Ministers. However, he was at odds with the majority of the Derg on several major issues. Aman thought the Derg was too large and unwieldy to function efficiently as a governing body. He also wanted to see peace made with Eritrea, and he urged reconciliation with its rebels.

Student and labor groups became increasingly opposed to the Derg. They demanded the formation of a "people's government" in which various national groups would be represented. The Derg clamped down on the dissidents who supported the people's demands. Meanwhile, Aman fell from grace with the Derg and it pressed charges against him. He was killed as he resisted arrest on November 23, a day that came to be known as Bloody Saturday. On that day, 59 political prisoners were executed, among them many prominent citizens and Derg members who had supported Andom.

Following the events of Bloody Saturday, Major Mengistu Haile Mariam retained the position of first vice chairman of the PMAC. From this point onward, Mengistu emerged as the leading force in the Derg. Now following the socialist path, the Derg announced in March 1975 that all royal titles were revoked and that the constitutional monarchy was to be abandoned. In August, Haile Selassie died in questionable circumstances while under house arrest. One of the last major links with Ethiopia's imperial past was broken in February 1976, when the patriarch of the Ethiopian Orthodox Church was deposed.

The Derg put forth its goals in greater detail in the Program for the National Democratic Revolution (PNDR). These goals included progress toward socialism under the leadership of workers, peasants, and all anti-imperialist forces. The Derg also wanted to create a one-party political system. Slogans such as "self-reliance," "the dignity of labor," and "the supremacy of the common good," embodied the Derg's brand of Ethiopian socialism. These slogans were devised to combat the widespread disdain of manual labor and a deeply rooted concern with status.

Land reform played a key role in Ethiopian socialism. Although everyone agreed that there was a need for land reform, few Ethiopians, even within the Derg, could agree on just how that reform should be accomplished. The Derg adopted a radical approach. It nationalized all rural land, abolished tenancy, and put peasants in charge of enforcement. No family could work a plot larger than 10 hectares (roughly 25 acres). No one could employ farm workers.

Farmers were expected to form peasant associations, which would enforce the new orders. This caused a great deal of disruption in rural areas. All urban land and apartments were also nationalized into urban dwellers' associations called *kebeles*.

The Derg also nationalized all banks and insurance firms and seized control of every important company in Ethiopia. Only wholesale and retail trade and import-export businesses remained in private hands. These moves cost the government a great deal of support from Ethiopia's left wing, which had been left out of the decision-making process. Students and teachers were also alienated by the government's closure of the university in Addis Ababa and all secondary schools in September 1975.

The transition from imperial to military rule was difficult and turbulent. The Derg faced powerful dissent from various groups in the country. In 1977, Mengistu declared himself chairman of the Derg. A serious challenge to the revolutionary government also occurred that year from events outside of the country. Somalia sought to regain the Ogaden, an area of Ethiopia it had once controlled. A Somali guerrilla organization attacked Ethiopian government positions throughout the Ogaden. The Somali government provided supplies and logistical support to the guerrilla organization. The group made steady progress, capturing large areas of Ethiopian territory in the region.

The fighting became more and more intense. Finally, in desperation, the Mengistu regime called on the Soviet Union for assistance. The Soviet Union previously had been supplying equipment and advisors in the hope of gaining influence in Ethiopia. Until the Soviets began to help Ethiopia, they had been supporting Somalia. The switch so outraged the Somalis that they expelled all Soviet advisors and ended the Treaty of Friendship and Cooperation they had with Moscow.

Mengistu Haile Mariam, chairman of the Coordinating Committee of the Armed Forces, Police, and Territorial Army (the Derg), which seized power from Haile Selassie in 1974, led Ethiopia after the revolution.

Beginning in late November 1977, massive Soviet military assistance began to pour into Ethiopia. Cuban troops stationed in Angola arrived to help the Ethiopian units. By 1978, Ethiopian and Cuban troops had driven the Somalis back toward the border. The Somali government then decided to withdraw its forces from the Ogaden, leaving the Ethiopian army in control of the region.

Even though the Ethiopian government developed a close relationship with the Communist world, the Soviets and their allies had many difficulties working with Mengistu and the Derg. Many of these problems resulted from members of the Derg's concern over internal matters and the promotion of Ethiopian variations of socialism. The Derg's status as a military government was another source of concern. Ethiopia's Communist allies made an issue of the need to create a civilian party that would rule a people's republic. To fulfill this request, the Derg formed the Commission to Organize the Party of the Workers of Ethiopia (COPWE), with Mengistu as its chairman.

A genuine Communist party replaced COPWE. Established in 1984, it was called the Workers' Party of Ethiopia. A new constitution submitted to the general public for suggestions and debate was finally approved in 1987. The task of publicizing this new constitution was assigned to the *kebeles* and peasant associations. Many people believed that these organizations served a government security role as well as local administrative duties. They were upset that very little open discussion or dissent was possible under these circumstances. Many people felt that the proposed constitution failed to address or even understand Ethiopian needs. In fact, some critics claimed that the document was little more than a revised version of the Soviet Constitution.

In September 1987, after 13 years of military rule, Ethiopia officially became the Peoples' Democratic Republic of Ethiopia (PDRE) under a new constitution that provided for a civilian government. The Ethiopian people elected the National Shengo (National Assembly). Many members of the now-defunct Derg continued to run Ethiopia's government, but with different titles. Despite outward appearances, little changed in the way the country was actually governed.

In 1991, the Soviet Union collapsed and the Cold War competition for power between Communist and free countries ended. No longer were many nations, such as Ethiopia, pawns in the struggle that had existed for almost 50 years. These and other changes would have a great impact on Ethiopia.

Despite the many advances Ethiopia's governments have tried to bring to the country, in rural areas, the people still follow many of the same customs they have used for centuries. These women, for example, still collect water in containers that they carry on their heads back to their homes.

5

People and Culture

E thiopians are a very diverse people. There are more than 100 different ethnic groups. Each group speaks one of more than 70 different languages found throughout the country. Ethnically, the Amhara, Tigray, and Oromo are Ethiopia's largest groups. They live primarily in the country's highlands. A fourth major group, the Somali, live in the southeastern lowlands.

With the accession of Menelik II to the throne in 1899, the ruling class consisted mainly of the Amhara, a predominantly Christian group that constitutes about 30 percent of the country's population. The Amhara are not a cohesive nor a close-knit ethnic group. In fact, Amhara from one area view those from other areas as quite different. There is a long history of conflict among Amhara nobles aspiring to be kings or kingmakers. During the imperial regime, Amhara dominance led to the adoption of Amharic as the language of government, commerce, and education. Amhara influence also was felt in local government, where Amhara served as representatives of the central government. The only region not dominated by the Amhara was Tigray, home of the people who lay claim to the Aksumite heritage.

The Oromo constitute about 40 percent of the population, but traditionally have not been as powerful as the Amhara. In terms of religion, the group is almost equally divided between Orthodox Christians and Muslims. The predominantly Christian Tigray occupy the far northern highlands and make up 12 to 15 percent of the population. They or their Eritrean neighbors have been fighting with the Ethiopian government for almost three decades and have achieved many battlefield successes.

POPULATION

According to estimates based on projections from Ethiopia's first official census in 1984, the country's population was 51.7 million in 1990. However, this census was not very comprehensive. Most rural areas of Eritrea and Tigray were excluded because of hostilities. Some areas could only give estimates of their population because of widely scattered settlement, including the prevalence of nomads. Ethiopia's 2002 population was estimated to be between 65 and 66 million. Population estimates for Ethiopia take into account the effects of excess mortality due to AIDS. AIDS can result in lower life expectancy, higher death rates and infant mortality rates, lower population growth rates, and changes in the distribution of population by age and sex than would otherwise be expected. Ethiopia's annual population growth rate was estimated to be approximately 2.9 percent in 2002, placing it well above the world average of 1.3 percent.

Nearly 45 percent of Ethiopia's population is under 15 years of age. Life expectancy in the country is just 52 years, with only two years separating males, with a life expectancy of 51, from females, with an expectancy of 53. The total fertility rate—the number of children to which the average woman will give birth—is estimated to be between six and seven. Census findings indicated that the birth rate was higher in rural than in urban areas. Ethiopia's rate of population growth is high even among developing countries. This can be explained by several factors. Many Ethiopians marry at a very young age, and almost everyone marries. Kinship ties and religious beliefs generally encourage large families. There is also strong resistance to contraceptive practices, and most of the population does not have access to family planning services. Many Ethiopians also believe that families with many children have greater financial security and are better able to provide for their elderly members.

The death rate is estimated to be 15 per 1,000 people, a figure that has been nearly the same for more than a decade. This rate is high, but is quite typical of many poor, less developed countries. The high death rate reflects a low standard of living, inferior health conditions, inadequate health facilities, and high rates of infant mortality and child mortality. Additional factors contributing to the high death rate include infectious diseases, poor sanitation, malnutrition, and food shortages. Children are especially vulnerable to such deprivations. In Ethiopia, half of all deaths involve children under five years of age. Drought and famine during the 1980s took a terrible toll on the population. More than 7 million people needed food aid, and many—perhaps one million—died of starvation. Because of inadequate diets, many children's physical and mental growth was stunted.

Generally, birth rates, infant mortality rates, and overall mortality rates were lower in urban areas than in rural areas. The wider availability of health facilities, better sanitation, more reliable access to food and clean water, and a higher standard of living help explain the more favorable statistics for urban areas.

Ethiopia continues to have a very high infant and child mortality rate. Children do not survive for many reasons, including drought, malnutrition, and diseases.

PATTERNS OF SETTLEMENT

Settlement is a concept that describes where and how people live. The 1984 census revealed that Ethiopia's population was about 89 percent rural and 11 percent urban. Since then, these percentages have changed little. In 2002, an estimated 85 percent of the population was rural and 15 percent urban.

The Ethiopian people have always been predominantly rural. In the highlands, they engage in agricultural activities such as farming and raising livestock. In the lowlands, the main activities traditionally have been subsistence farming by semi-nomadic groups and seasonal grazing of livestock by nomadic people.

The distribution of Ethiopia's population is related to elevation, climate, and soil. These physical factors explain the concentration of population in the highlands, which have moderate temperatures, rich soils, and adequate rainfall. About 14 percent of the population lives above 7,500 feet (2,300 meters) in the cool climatic zone. About 75 percent of the population lives in the temperate zone between 5,000 and 7,500 feet (1,500 to 2,300 meters). Only 11 percent lives below 5,000 feet in the scorching hot climatic zone, despite the fact that this area makes up more than half of Ethiopia's territory. Localities with elevations above 10,000 feet (3,000 meters) are cold and marked by rugged terrain, both of which limit agricultural activity. Areas below 5,000 feet in elevation are also sparsely settled because of high temperatures and very low rainfall, except in the west and southwest.

RELIGION

Before the 1974 revolution, Ethiopian Orthodox Christianity was the national religion of Ethiopia. The 1955 constitution stated that the Ethiopian Orthodox Church, founded in the fourth century on the doctrines of St. Mark, was the established church of the Ethiopian Empire and was, as such, supported by the state. The church supported both the state and the monarchy, and became part of the ethnic identity of the dominant Amhara and Tigray.

By contrast, Islam spread among ethnically diverse and geographically dispersed groups at different times. It therefore failed to provide the same degree of political unity for its members. Members of the Ethiopian Orthodox Church made up 40 to 50 percent of the population, including a majority of the Amhara and Tigray. Islam was the faith of about 40 percent of the population, including large segments of the Oromo and the people of the northern and eastern lowlands. Followers of native belief systems can also be found in Ethiopia. They are concentrated in remote areas bordering the western highlands and in scattered lowland regions. Many of the traditional beliefs and rituals were also part of the Christian and Muslim belief systems. Some rituals and beliefs, such as fear of the evil eye, were widespread among followers of all religions. The 1975 regime declared that all religions were equally legitimate. It made several Muslim holy days national holidays, in addition to the Eastern Orthodox holidays that were already observed.

Recent statistical data on religious affiliation is unreliable. Most Orthodox Christians are Amhara and Tigray. When members of these two groups are combined with others who have accepted Orthodoxy, the total Christian population might presently equal 50 percent of Ethiopians. Today, the Somali is the largest ethnic group associated with Islam. There are a few converts to Roman Catholicism and Protestantism.

CHRISTIAN ORTHODOXY

The Ethiopian Orthodox religion combined elements of Christianity and animist (native beliefs in spirits that are separate from physical bodies) religions. Christ is regarded as a divine aspect of the trinitarian (three-person) God. Angels and saints are also elements of Ethiopian Christianity. A hierarchy of angelic messengers and saints carries the prayers of the faithful to God and also performs God's divine will. When Ethiopian Christians have a problem, they pray to the saints and angels as well as to God. In more formal rituals, priests communicate with God on behalf of the faithful. Only priests may enter the inner sanctum of the church, where the ark of the church's patron saint is located. On important religious holidays, the ark is carried on the head of a priest and is escorted in a procession outside the church. The ark, not the church, is considered sacred. Only those who feel pure, have fasted regularly, and have behaved properly may enter the middle ring to take communion. At many services, the parish members remain in the outer ring.

Weekly services are only a small part of the life of a faithful and devout Ethiopian Orthodox Christian. Several holy days require prolonged services that include singing, dancing, and feasting. Another important religious requirement is the keeping of fast days. Only the clergy and the very devout keep the full schedule of fasts, which involve 250 days of the year. However, members of the church must fast for 165 days a year, including every Wednesday and Friday, and the two months that include Lent and the Easter season.

Timkat is the largest Christian festival celebrated in Ethiopia. It commemorates John's baptism of Jesus Christ in the Jordan River. During celebrations in churches through Ethiopia, the sacred *tabots*, or replicas of the Ark of the Covenant, are carried on the priests' heads into the central square of Gonder. Crowds of dancing people surround the sacred *tabots* as they are carried to their destination. Families gather in the garden surrounding the palace sanctuary to prepare special foods and drink special beer brewed locally for the Timkat festival. In Gonder, at precisely at 5:00 A.M. the next morning, the people jump into the icy cold waters of Fasilida's Pool for a mass baptism as the priests chant and pray.

In addition to standard holy days and the annual Timkat festival, most Christians also observe saint's days. A man might give a small feast on his personal saint's day. Each church honors its patron saint with a special service and feast two or three times a year.

Most Ethiopians believe in the existence of spirits—both

good and evil. Certain spirits called *zar* can be male or female, and possess a variety of personality traits. Many peasants believe they can prevent misfortune by pleasing the *zar*. The protective *adbar* spirits belong to the community, rather than to the families or individuals. The female *adbar* is thought to protect the community from disease, poverty, and misfortune. The male *adbar* is thought to prevent feuds, fighting, and war, and to bring about good harvests. People usually pay tribute to the *adbars* by bringing offerings of honey, grains, and butter. These practices are strongly discouraged by priests because the spirits are believed to be evil rather than religious.

There are many myths associated with the evil eye (*buda*). Most Ethiopians think that the ability to use this power is held by members of lower occupational groups who interact with the Amhara communities, but are not part of them. To prevent the effects of the evil eye, people wear amulets, or invoke God's name. Because one can never be sure of the source of an ailment or misfortune, a peasant can visit wizards who make diagnoses and specify cures. Wizards also make amulets or charms to ward off evil spirits and satanic creatures.

ISLAM

Ethiopian Muslims are adherents of the dominant Sunni, or orthodox, branch of Islam. The Shia branch of the faith is not represented in Ethiopia. The beliefs and practices of Ethiopian Muslims combine many influences. Most important, of course, are teachings of the Islamic holy book, the Koran, and the traditions of *sharia*, the law of Islam. Also important are the worship of saints, the rituals and organization of religious orders, and animistic beliefs. The traditional form of Islam is found only on the Eritrean coast among Arab and Arab-influenced populations and in a few towns such as Harar in Ethiopia's Eastern Province. The most important Muslim practices of regular prayer and fasting during the month of Ramadan are observed in urban centers rather than in smaller towns and villages, and more among settled peoples than among nomads.

Under Haile Selassie, Muslim communities could bring personal matters of family and inheritance before Islamic courts. However, many Muslims brought these matters to the Ethiopian courts. For example, the Somalis and other farmers and herders did not usually follow the requirement that daughters inherit half as much property as sons, especially when livestock was involved.

ETHIOPIAN CALENDAR

Ethiopia uses the Julian calendar, which is divided into 12 months of 30 days each and a thirteenth month of five or six days at the end of the year. The Ethiopian calendar is seven years and eight months behind the Gregorian calendar used in most Western nations. Once every four years, a leap day is added to this extra month to make it six days, making the average year 365-1/4 days long. Days begin at sunset. Unlike countries that use the Gregorian calendar, the first month of the year in Ethiopia is September and the last month right before the thirteenth month is August. The thirteenth month is called Paguemen, and is only five days long (six in a leap year). Time is also counted differently than in the Gregorian system. A day starts at 1:00 A.M. and ends 12:59 A.M.

EDUCATION AND LITERACY

Until the early 1900s, formal education in Ethiopia was limited to a system of religious instruction conducted by the Ethiopian Orthodox Church. Church schools prepared individuals for the clergy and to fill other church needs. In the process, these schools also provided religious education to the children of the nobility and to the sons of the tenant farmers and servants associated with elite families. Toward the end of the nineteenth century, several European mission-ary schools had been established as well. A small number of Islamic schools also provided some education for a small portion of the Muslim population.

By the start of the twentieth century, it had become obvious to the Ethiopian government that its failure to educate the population was taking a sharp toll in areas of government, diplomacy, commerce, and industry. As a result, the government began to introduce public education. The first public school was established in Addis Ababa in 1907, and a year later, an elementary school opened in Harar. A select number of students learned basic mathematics, foreign languages, and science, all taught in French. Amharic and religious subjects were also taught.

In 1925, the government adopted a plan to expand secular education, but 10 years later, there were only 8,000 students enrolled in 20 public schools. A few students also studied abroad on government scholarships. Schools were closed during the Italian occupation of 1936–1941. After Ethiopia regained its independence, schools were reopened. However, teachers, textbooks, and facilities were in drastically short supply. The government began to recruit foreign teachers for elementary and secondary schools to offset the teacher shortage. The U.S. Peace Corps and the National Service Program (made up of university students who taught for one year after completing their junior year) served as stopgap measures. Few teachers stayed long in the profession.

By 1952, a total of 60,000 students were enrolled in 400 elementary schools, 11 secondary schools, and three institu-tions offering college-level courses. In the 1960s, the country's public school system was supplemented by an additional 310 mission and privately operated schools with an enrollment of more than 50,000 students.

In the early 1960s, the government adopted a new education

policy that remained in effect until 1974. The policy empha-
sized the creation of technical training schools, but also
expanded traditional basic education as well. However, the
government made Amharic the language of instruction in
the elementary schools. This proved to be a major stumbling
block for the many children whose primary language was
not Amharic. There were two institutions of higher learning
in Ethiopia at this time—Haile Selassie I University in
Addis Ababa, founded in 1961, and the private University
of Asmera, an institution founded by a Roman Catholic
religious order based in Italy.

By 1974, in spite of government efforts to improve the
situation, less than 10 percent of the total population was
literate. There were several reasons for this lack of
progress. The chief reason for the failure of the education
system was its inability to respond to the needs of the
majority of the Ethiopian people. The system was rigid
and inflexible, and it was aimed at improving the education and needs of the elite, rather than those of the
general population. Money was also a problem. Only a
few major cities received adequate funding to achieve
their educational goals. Most people living in rural areas
remained out of reach of the educational system, and were
totally illiterate. By 1960, the Ethiopian educational
system ranked at the very bottom among the African
nations. There was a high dropout rate, severe school and
teacher shortages, and low overall attendance. The problem
was particularly critical among females, non-Christians,
and rural children.

By 1975, the provisional military government had overthrown imperial rule and instituted a series of reforms, some
of which were aimed at improving the educational system.
All private schools, except church-affiliated ones, were
nationalized and brought into the public school system.
Rural schools were improved as a way of increasing worker

productivity in the socialist mold. Haile Selassie I University was reorganized and renamed Addis Ababa University. However, no real education took place from 1975 to 1978, due to the country's social turmoil.

The revolutionary government did have one stunning educational success. It undertook a national literacy campaign. Before it came to power, the literacy rate was less than 10 percent. According to government figures, by 1984, it had increased to about 63 percent (although non-government sources estimated the literacy rate to have been closer to 37 percent). In 1991, some government reports were still reporting an adult literacy rate of more than 60 percent. This figure must be viewed with caution for two reasons. First, the military government wanted to report literacy rates that were as high as possible in order to gain public support, and second, the definition of literacy itself can be debated.

In 1979, a national committee was created to coordinate a nationwide literacy program. According to government sources, about 1.5 million people worked in this campaign. Among those who offered their free services to combat illiteracy were housewives, students, teachers, military personnel, and members of religious groups. Adult literacy classes used elementary and secondary school facilities in many areas. Officials distributed more than 22 million reading booklets and texts for both beginning and advanced readers. The Ministry of Education provided books on agriculture, health, and basic technology. For its efforts, United Nations Educational, Scientific, and Cultural Organization (UNESCO) awarded Ethiopia the International Reading Association Literacy Prize in 1980. Despite these efforts, today, however, it is estimated that Ethiopia's overall literacy rate is now only around 35 percent. Among males it is about 45 percent and among females 25 percent. Clearly, Ethiopia still has a long way to go toward educating its population.

HEALTH CARE

The people of Ethiopia suffer from many health problems. There are several reasons for this: Many people live in very remote areas, far away from any health care; widespread illiteracy prevents the easy spread of information about modern health practices; and health services are unevenly distributed because of a shortage of funds and trained health-care specialists.

Western medicine came to Ethiopia in the last quarter of the nineteenth century. Missionary doctors, nurses, and midwives came to help the people. However, there was little progress in the overall treatment of the many diseases that afflicted large numbers of Ethiopians. Finally, the government established the Ministry of Public Health in 1948. Many other international organizations, such as the World Health Organization (WHO) and the United Nations Children's Fund (UNICEF), provided technical and financial assistance to help eliminate the sources of health problems.

Beginning in 1974, Ethiopia introduced a new health policy that stressed disease prevention and control, rural health services, and the promotion of community involvement in health activities. Health care was also decentralized, giving local communities a stronger voice in health related matters. Many new hospitals and clinics were built. Programs were introduced to train Ethiopian health-care personnel to staff the new facilities. By 1989, however, these facilities were available to only a small fraction of Ethiopia's people. An estimated 80 percent of the population still did not have access to adequate medical care.

As was the case in most developing countries in the early 1990s, Ethiopia's main health problems were communicable diseases caused by poor sanitation and malnutrition. Nearly 60 percent of childhood deaths were preventable. Causes of death included diarrhea, upper respiratory illnesses, malnutrition, and fevers. Tuberculosis still affected much of the population despite efforts to immunize as many people as possible. Venereal diseases were prevalent, especially in towns where prostitution contributed to the problem.

Ethiopia's first reported case of HIV was reported in 1984, and the first confirmed case of acquired immunodeficiency syndrome (AIDS) appeared in 1986. By 1990, AIDS was reported to be spreading rapidly in heavily traveled areas. In rural areas, the prevalence of the human immunodeficiency virus (HIV)—the precursor of full-blown AIDS—in the adult population increased from 2.7 percent in 1989 to 7.3 percent in 2000. In urban areas, HIV prevalence is much higher, at 13.4 percent. Even so, the number of reported cases of AIDS in Ethiopia is smaller than in many other African countries. This is believed, however, to be because fewer resources were devoted to tracking and reporting the diseases in Ethiopia than in other countries.

FAMILY LIFE AND THE ROLE OF WOMEN

Ethiopian families are very strong. They tend to be large, and divide the work among fathers, mothers, and children. Family size will surely be reduced as education improves and employment opportunities increase. Traditionally, however, fathers work in the fields, while mothers work in the home, where they tend to the children and care for the household's needs. Large extended families, including many relatives, often live within a single family compound.

In Ethiopian families, the emphasis is on the family group, rather than on individual members. People also belong to larger social groups, though, which are especially significant during ceremonies and rituals associated with marriage and burial. Weddings and funerals are very important events in the life of Ethiopians. There are usually large numbers of guests and great quantities of food and drink at these ceremonies.

Ethiopian women experience tremendous physical hardships throughout their lives. They carry heavy loads over long distances, grind corn manually, work in the home and fields, raise the children, and do most of the cooking and cleaning for the family. As in other traditional societies, a woman's worth is measured by the way she fulfills her role as wife and mother. Over 85 percent of Ethiopian women reside in rural areas, where peasant families engage in subsistence agriculture. Rural life takes a toll on women and children. The revolution of the 1970s did not better the lives of rural women. Land reform did not change their inferior status, which was based on deeply rooted traditional values and beliefs. An improvement in economic conditions would improve the standard of living of Ethiopian women, but real change would require much more. It would require a change in the attitudes of the government and men regarding women in Ethiopian society.

In urban areas, health care, education, and employment are more readily available to women and children. Although a few women with higher education have found professional employment, most hold low-paying jobs. About 40 percent of employed women in urban areas work in the service sector, where they hold jobs in hotels, restaurants, and bars. Women workers still earn a small fraction—usually less than half—of the wages men earn for the same type of labor. These differences in wages exist even though the government issued a proclamation as long ago as 1975 that said men and women must receive equal wages for equal work.

After the revolution, women made some gains in political and economic areas. More women are being educated today than ever before. Women's organizations have formed in factories and the civil service. Some women participate in local organizations and in peasant associations and *kebeles*.

Unfortunately, the role of women continues to be limited at the national level, and most of the progress that has been made has occurred in the urban centers.

URBAN SOCIETY

Ethiopia is one of the world's most rural countries. Only about 15 percent of its people live in urban areas. Hundreds of communities have 2,000 to 5,000 people, but these are mainly extensions of rural villages that have no urban or administrative functions. Therefore, the level of urbanization would be even lower if one used strict criteria.

The reason Ethiopia lacks cities is because of its agricultural self-sufficiency. This history of self-sufficiency in food production has reinforced Ethiopia's rural peasant life. Urbanization did begin to increase during the 1960s, however, particularly in northern Ethiopia where most of the major towns are located.

Only after World War II did towns and the commerce on which they depend become very significant in Ethiopia. Towns were generally small (except for Addis Ababa and some Red Sea ports). Urbanization here occurred more slowly than in other African countries (about one-third of the continent of Africa, as a continent, is urbanized). City and town life was not a feature of Ethiopian society, and trade was not a full-time occupation for most Ethiopians.

Manufacturing was a recent arrival and Ethiopians played a very small role in industry. For the most part, foreigners filled managerial positions. Even today, manufacturing employs less than one percent of the labor force. The country has an abundance of unskilled and semi-skilled laborers. There is a serious shortage of people trained to be managers or supervisors, or to work in highly skilled specialized fields such as medicine and engineering. Most industry is concentrated in a few regions of the country. Addis Ababa is the primary center of manufacturing, commerce, and services.

Secondary centers include the Shewa region, Dire Dawa, and the Harar region. More than 90 percent of the country's measured (cash, rather than barter or self-sufficient) economic wealth is produced in these four centers.

Addis Ababa, home to an estimated 2.5 million people, holds more than one-third of Ethiopia's urban population. The city is located at the geographic center of the country, in the mountainous Shawa Province. It is Ethiopia's chief political, economic, and cultural center, as well as its largest city.

Between 1967 and 1975, several fairly new urban centers grew rapidly. Many small towns began to emerge, and by 1980, there were 229 small towns scattered around Ethiopia. Awasa, Arba Minch, Metu, and Goba were newly designated capitals of administrative regions, and important agricultural centers. Awasa, capital of the Sidamo region, had a lakeshore site and convenient location on the Addis Ababa–Nairobi highway. Bahir Dar was a newly planned city on Lake Tana and the site of several industries and a polytechnic institute. Akaki and Aseb became important industrial towns, while Jijiga and Shashemene had become communications and service centers. Most of the moderate growth was experienced in older, more established towns such as Addis Ababa and Debre Zeyit. A few old provincial towns, such as Gonder, also experienced moderate growth, but others, such as Harer, Dese, and Jima, had slow growth rates because of competition from larger cities.

Overall, the rate of urban growth declined from 1975 to 1987. Several factors can explain this. The rapid expansion of urban centers during the period of 1967–1975 was largely fueled by rural-to-urban migration. Between 1975 and 1984, natural population increase probably caused the growth spurt. The 1975 land reform program provided incentives and opportunities for peasants to stay in rural areas. Restrictions on travel, lack of jobs, housing shortages, and urban unrest may have slowed the rural-to-urban migration during 1975–1980. Between 1988 and 1991, intensified warfare forced all urban centers to receive a large number of people who were fleeing the hostilities. This influx of people caused a severe housing and water shortage, over-taxed social services, and created terrible overcrowding in urban centers. In addition to beggars and maimed persons, the new arrivals comprised large numbers of young people. Many were street children and orphans of the war. Addis Ababa, as Ethiopia's capital, was most affected by this huge wave of internal migration.

INTERESTING AND IMPORTANT PLACES

Although Ethiopia faces dire conditions in many areas, it also has many positive aspects. Ethiopia's natural beauty often amazes the first-time visitor. It is a land of rugged mountains, broad savannas, sparkling lakes, rushing rivers, and parched deserts. The Great Rift Valley is a remarkable region of volcanic lakes famous for their collections of birds, bold cliffs, and stunning views. Falls on the Blue Nile River are spectacular. Ethiopia has 14 major wildlife reserves where one can observe—in miniature—nearly all the ecosystems found elsewhere in Africa. Bird, fish, and other animal life abounds.

Ethiopia boasts many natural tourist attractions. There are islands in Lake Tana with fifteenth-century monasteries, one of which can only be visited by men. The mural paintings in the churches there represent beautiful pieces of religious art. The monks care for religious artifacts and manuscripts, written in Gi'iz on goat and horse skin. Nearby Bahir Dar is a city of many shop, bars, and small hotels. Musicians play harps and sing traditional Ethiopian music in many of the cafes.

Gonder was Ethiopia's capital city from 1666 to 1864. Emperor Fasilada founded it and built the many beautiful palaces there. Outside Gonder, in the valley of Qaha, he built

Gonder is one of Ethiopia's most interesting sites to visit. Once the capital of the nation, Gonder is home to many beautiful castles, such as this one, built by King Fasilada.

a palace overlooking a bath called Emperor Fasilada's bath. His successors followed his example and built smaller castles within the same compound that is surrounded by basalt walls. Fasilada's grandson built the Church of Debre Birha Selassie, called the Abbey of the Light of Trinity. Wonderful mural paintings grace the walls and ceilings of this abbey.

Deep in the Ethiopian highlands lies the little town of Lalibela (originally called Roha). This community was the capital of the Zagwe dynasty, which ruled over Ethiopia from the tenth to the mid-thirteenth century. King Lalibela ordered 13 magnificent churches carved out of the rock of Lalibela. Saints and other mystical symbols grace the walls of these churches. Lalibela is often called the eighth wonder of the world. The legend of Lalibela says that King Lalibela's older brother poisoned him. During a three-day sleep, he was brought to heaven, where he was shown a city of rock-hewn churches that he later replicated. Other stories say that King Lalibela went into exile in Jerusalem, where he received a vision that told him to create a new Jerusalem. A small gorge called the River Jordan and a tomb of Abraham are carved from solid rock. A pillar covered with cotton stands in one of the churches. One of the monks said he once saw Jesus Christ kissing the pillar. Tunnels and small passages connect the 13 churches to one another.

Ethiopian Muslims consider Harer a holy city and the fourth most important city of Islam. Within its walls there are 90 mosques. It was founded in the twelfth century, and in 1520, was captured by Muslim invader Ahmed Gragn, who used Harer as a base from which to invade large portions of Ethiopia. In 1875, the Egyptians captured Harer, and in 1887, Menelik II took control of it and appointed Ras Makonnen, the father of Haile Selassie, as its governor. The French poet Rimbaud lived in Harer as a trader. Many large and small markets can be found both inside and outside the city. For a few dollars, tourists can watch men feeding wild hyenas in the evening. Harer is a colorful and lively city.

The ancient Romans described Axum as "the greatest city of all Ethiopia." Early historical references say that ancient Axum was a major cosmopolitan urban center. By the sixth century, Axum had become the most important power between the Roman Empire and Persia. It sent its merchant navies as far away as Egypt, India, Ceylon, and China. It adopted

Christianity as its state religion as early as the fourth century. The Ark of the Covenant reportedly is kept here in a small chapel adjacent to a very old church. The city is best known for its well-preserved ancient obelisks that are carved of solid granite. Some of the obelisks are more than 2,000 years old, attesting to a high level of advancement in art and architecture at a date far earlier than that of any other civilization in sub-Saharan Africa. The largest of these stelae is reported to have collapsed to the ground 1,000 years ago. It weighed over 500 tons and stood 110 feet tall. It was thought to have been the largest single piece of stone ever successfully quarried and erected in the ancient world. Other towering stone stelae are 70 feet high and covered with elaborate carvings.

Another interesting region is Afar. It stretches from the city of Awash north to the Denakil Depression and crosses the borders with Eritrea and Djibouti. A well-maintained road connects Awash with the harbors of Asab and Djibouti. This area of Ethiopia is tropical desert and water is scarce. The Muslim people who live here are largely nomadic, and live in small oval huts. They tend herds of goats, camels, and cattle. These people consider themselves Ethiopia's earliest inhabitants. The men carry large knives and sometimes rifles while traveling with their herds. Fights between rival tribes are not uncommon.

The main road from Addis Ababa to Kenya is called the Moyale Road. It is one of the few paved roads in Ethiopia. The road is full of people walking and riding bicycles. Ethiopia is a country where one typically needs a four-wheel drive vehicle to get around.

The Rift Valley is a beautiful green part of Ethiopia. Many lakes and hot springs make this region a popular vacation spot for Ethiopians. The land is fertile and there is plenty of water for farming. Farmers grow coffee, peppers, potatoes, and bananas here. The valley is one more part of Ethiopia's diverse landscape.

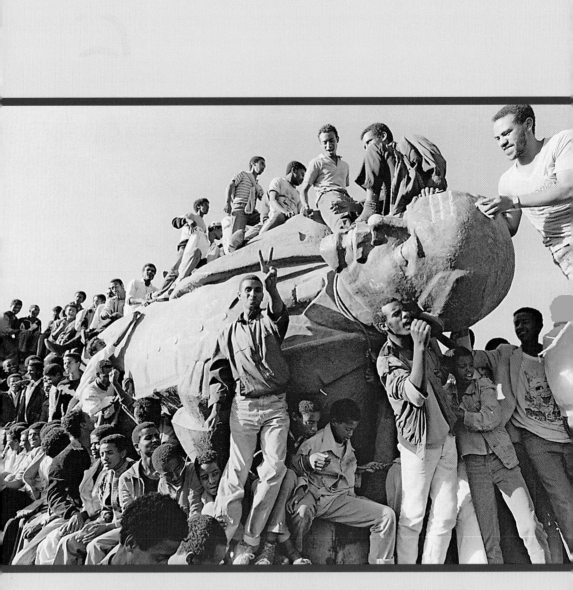

In 1991, the people rebelled against the socialist government instituted in the 1970s by the Derg. Here, a group of young Ethiopians stands on a toppled statue of Soviet leader Vladimir Lenin, which had been a symbol of the socialist government.

CHAPTER

6

Government

E thiopia's official name is the Federal Democratic Republic of Ethiopia. Its capital is the city of Addis Ababa. The country is unique among African states because it has managed to remain free from colonial rule, except for the brief Italian occupation of 1936–1941. It is the oldest independent country in Africa and one of the oldest countries in the world.

ETHIOPIA IN EARLIER YEARS

The ancient Ethiopian monarchy remained intact until a military coup deposed Emperor Haile Selassie in 1974. Following the coup, the new government established a socialist state. Two decades of bloody coups, uprisings, wide-scale drought, and massive refugee problems plagued the socialist government. It was finally toppled by a coalition of rebel forces called the Ethiopian People's Revolutionary Democratic Front (EPRDF) in 1991.

RECENT GOVERNMENT ISSUES

A new constitution was adopted in December 1994, and Ethiopia's first multiparty elections were held in 1995. Thus, the country has taken initial steps toward a democratic form of government.

The conflict with Eritrea continues. After a long and bloody conflict, Eritrea gained its independence from Ethiopia in 1993. But a border war between the two countries erupted in Eritrea in 1998. It has strengthened the ruling coalition, but has hurt Ethiopia's economy. Additionally, an estimated 70,000 to 120,000 soldiers and civilians have died in the ongoing conflict.

Ethiopia has nine ethnically based administrative regions and two chartered cities, Addis Ababa and Dire Dawa. The most important holiday is National Day, which takes place on May 28. This day marks the defeat of the socialist Mengistu regime in 1991.

HOW THE GOVERNMENT WORKS

Under Ethiopia's constitution, the government is headed by a prime minister. The council of ministers forms the cabinet. The cabinet members are appointed by the prime minister and approved by the House of People's Representatives. The House of People's Representatives elects the president for a six-year term. The president is commander and chief of the armed forces, and is responsible for implementing both domestic and foreign policies. The party in power following legislative elections selects a prime minister. Ministers are selected by the prime minister and approved by the House of People's Representatives. The prime minister presides over the council of ministers, and is responsible for normal administrative functions of government. These include forming laws and regulations, preparing the annual budget, and ensuring the social and economic well-being of the population.

The legislative branch of Ethiopia's government consists

Ethiopia celebrates "National Day" every May 28. The holiday marks the date in 1991 when the socialist Mengistu regime was overthrown.

The people of Ethiopia elect many of their government representatives. This woman is casting her ballot in the May 2000 elections in the city of Addis Ababa.

of a two-party Parliament. The upper chamber is called the House of Federation and the lower chamber is the House of People's Representatives. The House of Federation has 117 seats, which are filled by representatives chosen by state assemblies to serve five-year terms. The House of People's Representatives has 548 seats, which are filled by a direct popular vote of the people of each district.

The federal Supreme Court forms the judicial branch of the government. The president and vice president of the federal Supreme Court are recommended by the prime minister and appointed by the House of People's Representatives. Other federal judges are chosen by the federal Judicial Administrative Council and submitted to the House of People's Representatives for appointment.

POLITICAL PARTIES

Ethiopia has several large political parties, including the All-Amhara People's Organization or AAPO; the Coalition of Alternative Forces for Peace and Democracy or CAFPD; and the Ethiopian Democratic Union (EDU), to name just a few. Dozens of smaller political parties are also active in Ethiopia. Many small, ethnically based political pressure groups have formed since the defeat of the socialist regime in 1991. Among these parties are several Islamic militant groups.

Ethiopia's economy is based primarily on agriculture. The people grow many crops, including coffee and a wide variety of grains such as those seen here at the Dire Dawa market.

7

Economy

E thiopia is one of the most rural, agriculturally dependent countries on Earth. Approximately 85 percent of its people are rural, and about 90 percent of that rural population earns its living from the land. Most are subsistence farmers, who grow only what they need for their families.

Agriculture is the backbone of the national economy. The principal exports are coffee, oil seeds, pulses, flowers, vegetables, sugar, and foodstuffs for animals. There is also a growing livestock sector, which exports cattle on the hoof, as well as hides and skins.

The importance of agriculture to Ethiopia's economy is abundantly evident: Fully 90 percent of its exports, 80 percent of its direct and indirect employment, and approximately 50 percent of its gross domestic product (GDP) are based on agriculture. Unfortunately, the agricultural sector suffers from poor cultivation practices and frequent periods of drought. This leads to the result that, in a country where most people are involved in farming, nearly 5 million Ethiopians require food assistance each year to survive.

Ethiopia's economy has opened up since the government overthrow in 1991. This has led to the development of several natural resources. Ethiopia has reserves of coal, oil, natural gas, gold, potash, zinc, marble, and copper, as well as precious and semi-precious stones. Ethiopia is the "water tower" for the surrounding region. Plans are now in progress to develop Ethiopia's water resources for hydroelectricity generation and for increased agricultural production. Mineral exploration and mining have also increased in recent years.

In December 1999, Ethiopia signed a $1.4 billion joint venture to develop a huge natural gas field in the Somali Regional State. Conflict over Eritrea, however, has forced the government to scale back its ambitious development plans. Foreign investment has already declined significantly. The government imposed stiff taxes in 1999 to finance the Eritrean war. This served to depress an already weak economy. On the positive side, the war has forced the government to improve roads and other parts of the previously neglected rural infrastructure. This has benefited certain regions but not others.

AGRICULTURE

Coffee is critical to the Ethiopian economy. Ethiopia earned $267 million in 1999 by exporting 105,000 metric tons (231,485 pounds) of coffee. It is currently estimated that coffee contributes 10 percent of Ethiopia's GDP. More than 15 million people (25 percent of the population) derive their income either directly or indirectly from coffee. The coffee grown in Ethiopia is almost exclusively of the arabica type, which grows best at elevations between 3,000 and 6,000 feet (roughly 1,000 to 2,000 meters). Coffee grows wild in many parts of Ethiopia,

Coffee is Ethiopia's biggest cash crop. It makes up 90 percent of the nation's exports. A huge part of the population depends to some extent on coffee to make a living. This Ethiopian woman is grinding coffee beans in the traditional way.

although most Ethiopian coffee is deliberately cultivated in the southern and western regions of Kefa, Sidamo, Ilubabor, Gamo Gofa, Welega, and Harerge. The government, in its desire to increase hard-currency reserves, has discouraged the domestic consumption of coffee. It did this by controlling local coffee sales and by restricting the transfer of coffee from coffee-producing areas to other parts of the country. This practice made the price of coffee in Ethiopia two to three times higher than the price of exported coffee.

Ethiopia's chief food crops include a variety of cereals, pulses, and oilseeds. Grains are the most important field crops and the main element in the diet of most Ethiopians. The principal grains are teff, wheat, barley, corn, sorghum, and millet. Teff, wheat, and barley are primarily cool-weather crops cultivated at elevations above 4,000 feet. Teff, which is native to Ethiopia, is made into flour and used to make *injera*, the unleavened bread consumed in the highlands and urban centers throughout Ethiopia. Barley is mainly grown between 6,000 and 10,000 feet (1,828 and 3,048 meters). A major subsistence crop, barley is used as food and in the production of *tella*, a locally produced beer.

Sorghum, millet, and corn are grown mostly in warmer areas at lower elevations along the country's western, southwestern, and eastern borders. Sorghum and millet are drought-resistant, which means they can grow at lower elevations where rainfall is less reliable. Corn is grown mainly between elevations of 5,000 to 7,000 feet (1,524 and 2,133 meters)and requires large amounts of rainfall to ensure good harvests. These three grains constitute the staple foods of much of Ethiopia's population.

Pulses—beans, peas, lentils, and other pod crops—are the second most important element of the Ethiopian diet. They are a principal source of protein. Pulses are eaten boiled, roasted, or in stew. They grow at all elevations, from sea level to about 9,000 feet (2,743 meters), and are more prevalent in the northern and central highlands. Before the revolution, pulses were a chief export. The Ethiopian Orthodox Church traditionally has forbidden the consumption of animal fats on many days of the year. As a result, vegetable oils are widely used, making oilseed cultivation an important agricultural activity.

Ensete, or false banana, is an important food source in Ethiopia's southern and southwestern highlands. This plant resembles a banana, but bears an inedible fruit. Ensete, which produces an underground starchy plant stem, reaches a height of several meters. Locals use ensete to make the flour that is their staple food. Taro, yams, and sweet potatoes are commonly grown in the same region as ensete. Cultivated vegetables and fruit do not make up a large portion of an Ethiopian's diet because of their high cost. Common cultivated vegetables include onions, peppers, squash, and a cabbage similar to kale.

Because most of the lowlands lack sufficient rainfall, cotton cultivation depends largely on irrigation. Ethiopia is completely self-sufficient in cotton. This crop holds significant promise for export. The country's existing textile industries use approximately 50,000 tons of cotton annually. In addition, there are good prospects for exporting cotton lint, as well as opportunities for increasing production and processing of cotton.

Livestock production is an important part of Ethiopia's economy. Almost the entire rural population is involved in raising livestock. Animals pull loads, provide food, cash, transportation, fuel, and even social prestige in some rural communities. Beef accounts for at least half of all meat consumption, followed by lamb, poultry, and goat. Cattle in Ethiopia are almost entirely of the zebu type, and are poor sources of milk and meat. However, zebu do relatively well under Ethiopia's traditional production system. The majority of cattle in Ethiopia are raised in the highlands, with only about one-third raised in the lowlands. During the rainy season, when grass and water are plentiful, herds thrive. However, when the dry season sets in, forage is insufficient to keep herds well fed and able to resist disease. Consequently, droughts are as hard on cattle as they are on people.

Almost every farmstead raises poultry both for consumption and cash sale. Individual poultry farms provide eggs and

Finding water for people and crops is a very difficult task in Ethiopia, particularly in times of drought, which occur relatively frequently. In an attempt to solve this problem, Ethiopia has undertaken many irrigation projects that are intended to bring water from faraway sources to the areas that need it.

meat for urban dwellers. Small farmers raise sheep and goats for meat and for cash income. The majority of sheep flocks are found in the highland areas, whereas goats are predominantly raised in the lowlands. Both animals have high sale value in urban centers, especially around holidays such as Easter and New Year's Day.

FISHING

Ethiopia's many lakes, rivers, and reservoirs offer fertile fishing grounds. Even so, fishing contributes less than one percent of Ethiopia's GDP, and fish are not an important part of the diet of most Ethiopians. Seasonal demand for fish is usually based on religious influences. For example, Christians must abstain from meat, milk, and eggs during Lent, but they can eat fish at that time of year.

LAND USE AND REFORM

Inaccessibility, water shortages, and infestations of disease-causing insects prevent the use of large parcels of potentially productive land. In Ethiopia's lowlands, for instance, the presence of malaria has kept large numbers of farmers from settling in many areas. There are two main soil types found in the highlands. The first type, found in areas with good drainage, consists of reddish clay loam that holds moisture and contains many minerals. It is generally found in much of Ilubabor, Kefa, and Gamo Gofa. The second type of soil is a brownish-gray to black soil with high clay content. This soil is found in both the southern and northern highlands, in areas with poor drainage. It is sticky when wet, hard when dry, and generally difficult to work. However, with proper drainage and conditioning, both of these soils have tremendous agricultural potential. Sandy desert soils cover much of the arid lowlands in the northeast and in the Ogaden area of southeastern Ethiopia. Because of low rainfall, these areas have limited agricultural potential, except in areas where rainfall is sufficient for the growth of natural forage at certain times of the year. The Awash River basin supports many large-scale commercial farms and several irrigated small farms.

Soil erosion is one of Ethiopia's most severe environmental problems. Over the centuries, deforestation, overgrazing, and practices such as the cultivation of steep slopes have eroded the soil. In addition, the rugged topography of the highlands, the brief but extremely heavy rainfalls of many areas, and traditional farming methods have accelerated soil erosion in much of Ethiopia's highland areas. In the dry lowlands, constant winds also contribute to soil erosion.

RESETTLEMENT

In Ethiopia, a predominantly rural society, the life of peasants is rooted to the land from which they eke out a meager existence. Drought and famine have been frequent occurrences in Ethiopia. The imperial government's attempts to hide the effects of the severe famine of 1973–1974 from the world eventually led to Haile Selassie's downfall. Between 1984 and 1986, drought and famine hit Ethiopia again, and may have claimed as many as one million lives and threatened nearly 8 million others. The international community mounted a massive effort to airlift food and medical supplies to famine victims, and thus averted an even worse disaster.

Ethiopia's government began a program of forced resettlement and village building in the mid-1980s. It is part of a national attempt to combat drought, avert famine, and increase agricultural productivity. Resettlement was always the regime's long-term solution to the drought problem. It involved the permanent relocation of about 1.5 million people from the drought-prone areas of the north to the south and southeast, where the population was fairly sparse and arable land was plentiful.

Even though everyone agreed that there was a need to move famine victims, the actual resettlement was poorly planned and inefficiently conducted. Many people died and thousands of families were broken up. Thousands more died of malaria and sleeping sickness because of poor sanitation and inadequate health care in the newly settled areas. Doctors Without Borders, a Paris-based international doctors' organization, estimated that the forced resettlement and mass deportation of peasants endangered the lives of 300,000 people because of shortages of food, water, and medicine. Widespread criticism from many international organizations led the Mengistu regime to halt the resettlement program temporarily in mid-1986 after 600,000 people had been relocated. Critics claimed that the regime's main motive in resettlement was to depopulate the northern areas, where it faced rebellions.

Another objection to the resettlement program related to the long-term government policy concerning peasant farms. Western countries did not want to sponsor a plan in which recruits labored for Communist-style collectives and state farms. The Mengistu regime's argument for relocating peasants to larger villages was to provide them with better access to amenities such as schools, clinics, water, and electricity. The regime believed that improved economic and social services would lead to better use of land and other natural resources, higher agricultural productivity, and a higher standard of living.

Thousands of people fled to avoid being relocated in villages, while others died or lived in deplorable conditions after they were forcibly resettled. In the short term, resettlement in villages did not improve the lot of the peasants. The Ethiopian government lacked the resources to provide the services it had promised. The peasants had to travel farther to work on their land and graze their cattle, thus wasting their time and effort. They also lived too far from their fields to be able to protect them from wild animals and birds. In the long run, analysts believed that the creation of more villages would be counterproductive. The villages did not meet the needs of existing land use systems, and could also increase damage to the environment. Concentrating people in a central area would increase pressure on land and water supplies and lead to a decline in soil fertility. Ecological damage could be averted with capital outlays to build up the infrastructure, such as irrigation and land-intensive agricultural technology. Unfortunately, resources were not available for such development.

Although it faces many terrible problems as it tries to develop its economy and resources, Ethiopia is also a beautiful land of mountains, plains, and deserts.

CHAPTER

8

Ethiopia Looks to the Future

Ethiopia today is still mainly a rural society. The life of the people is rooted in the land. Through the ages, Ethiopians have faced frequent natural disasters, armed conflicts, and political repression. They have suffered hunger, disruption of their society, and often death. When seasonal rains fail or unusually heavy storms cause widespread flooding, crops are ruined and livestock is lost. Pastoral nomads, who move seasonally in search of water and grazing lands, are often trapped when drought inhibits grass production in their grazing areas. At such times, a family's food supplies may dwindle rapidly, and hunger and starvation become commonplace until weather conditions improve and livestock is healthy once again.

This has been the pattern of life for centuries in Ethiopia. Insurgent movements in Eritrea (which is no longer part of Ethiopia), Tigray, and the Ogaden have only served to exacerbate the effects of these natural disasters.

A drought that started in 1969 in the dry Sahel continued eastward into the Horn of Africa for five years. By 1973, thousands of Ethiopian refugees were pouring across the borders into neighboring Somalia, Sudan, Djibouti, and Kenya to avoid starvation. Thousands died, unable to escape the famines. The military regime that came into power in 1974 was unable to provide adequate help for the people. Conflicts in Tigray, Eritrea, and the Ogaden added to the refugee crisis. Even massive amounts of international aid were unable to provide sufficient relief for the people of Ethiopia. The makeshift refugee camps in neighboring countries were full of women and children. Many died of malnutrition, dehydration, and disease, as a lack of sanitation and inadequate medical help compounded the crisis.

By mid-1980, most observers considered the refugee crisis in the Horn of Africa the worst in the world. As the situation intensified, millions more of the area's people continued to flee their homes and to seek refuge in neighboring countries. Continuous civil wars, severe government repression, and resettlement programs added to the reasons refugees fled Ethiopia during the 1980s. International food aid was often hindered when insurgents and civil wars disrupted supply lines and food distribution convoys. The fighting destroyed airports and prevented the safe movement of food convoys over the rough, rutted roads.

Ethiopia's history does have its positive points, however. For more than 3,000 years, Ethiopia has been a land of mystery and fascination. The Greek poet Homer believed that the gods had blessed the Ethiopians. More recently, the famous African-American leader W.E.B.

Border conflicts with Eritrea, the neighboring country that was once part of Ethiopia, have led to a serious crisis as people fled to other nations to get away from the fighting. These people are Eritrean refugees who set up camp at Wad Sharif in Sudan in 1989.

DuBois described Ethiopia as "the all mother of men." Whatever Ethiopia's future holds, one thing is certain: Without peace and stability, economic development is

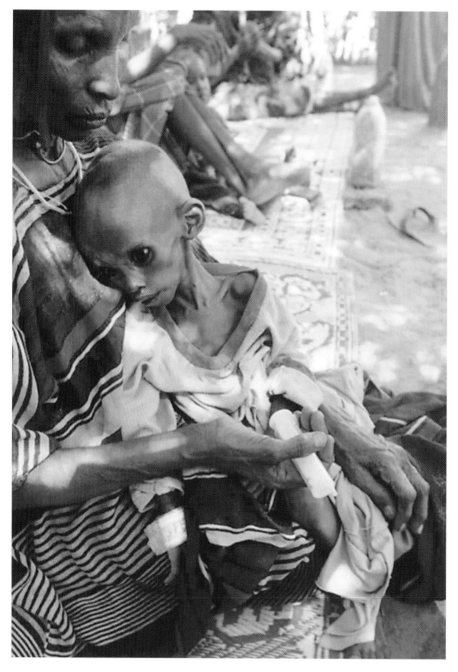

Malnutrition continues to claim the lives of large numbers of children, as well as adults, in Ethiopia. It is not uncommon to see disturbing sights such as this mother holding her starving child.

going to be very difficult for Ethiopia to achieve. Without a developed economy, there can be no meaningful application of modern science and technology that will better the lives of the people.

Facts at a Glance

Country Name	*Official*: Federal Democratic Republic of Ethiopia *Conventional*: Ethiopia
Location	Landlocked country in northeastern Africa, bordered by Sudan, Kenya, Somali, Djibouti, and Eritrea
Area	Approximately 472, 000 sq. miles (1.1 millions sq. km), Slightly less than twice the size of Texas
Capital	Addis Ababa
Terrain	Generally high, rugged volcanic plateau and mountainous, with arid lowland plains in south and east
Elevation Extremes	*Highest point*: Ras Dashen (Dejen) Terara, 15,571 feet (4,746 meters) *Lowest point:* Denakil Depression, -410 feet (-125 meters)
Land Use	Arable land, 12% Permanent crops, 1% Permanent pastures, 40% Forest and woodland, 25% Little economic activity, 22%
Climate	Tropical highlands and desert lowland plains. Great variations in both temperature and precipitation resulting differences in topography and elevation.
Water Features	Landlocked; several lakes occupying Great Rift Valley depressions; the Blue Nile, major tributary to the Nile, begins in Lake Tana in northwestern Ethiopia
Natural Hazards	Earthquakes, volcanic eruptions, frequent droughts, locusts plagues
Environmental Issues	Deforestation, overgrazing, soil erosion, and desertification
Population	65 to 66 million (2002 estimate)
Population Growth Rate	2.9% per year (2002 estimate)
Life Expectancy	*Total years:* 45 *Male:* 44 *Female:* 46
Ethnic Groups	Oromo, 40%; Amhara and Tigre, 32%; Sidamo, 9%; Shankella, 6%; Somali, 6%; other 7%
Religions	Muslim, 45-50%, Ethiopian Orthodox, 35-40%, Animist, 12%, other 3-8%

Languages	Amharic (official), Tigrinya, Oromifa, Somali, English (major foreign language taught in schools)
Literacy	*Total population:* 36% *Male:* 46% *Female:* 25%
Type of Government	Federal republic
Leadership	*Chief of state:*President (Elected by Houseof People's Representatives for a six-year term) *Head of state:* Prime Minister (Designated by party in power following legislative elections)
Administrative Divisions	9 ethnically-based states and 2 self-governing administrations
Independence	Oldest independent country in Africa and one of the oldest in the world, a least 2,000 years. Was never colonized.
GDP-Purchasing Power Parity	*National:* $39 billion (2001 estimate) *Per capita:* $620
Currency	Birr
Labor Force by Occupation	Agriculture, 80%; government and services, 12%; industry and construction, 8%
Exports	*Items:* Coffee, gold, leather product *Partners:* Germany (16%), Japan (13%), Djibouti (10%), Saudi Arabia (7%)
Imports	*Items:* Food, live animals, petroleum, chemicals, machinery, motor vehicles *Partners:* Saudi Arabia (28%), Italy (10%), Russia (7%), U.S.A. (6%)
Transportation	*Railways:* 425 miles (680 km) *Highways:* 15,000 miles (25,000 km) *Paved roads*: 2,000 miles (3,200 km)

Sources:
CIA, The World Factbook, Ethiopia
http://www.cia.gov/cia/publications/factbook/geos/et.html

U. S. Department of State, Background Notes, Ethiopia
http://www.state.gov/r/pa/ei/gbn/2859pf.htm

1523	Ethiopia repelled a Muslim invasion; developed as an isolated kingdom.
1850s	Egypt and Sudan kept sent troops into Ethiopia; Emperor Tewodros renews Ethiopia's political power; his successor, Menelik II, doubles size of Ethiopia.
1896	Italian invasion of Asmara repelled; Europeans recognize Ethiopia's independence.
1913	Menelik II dies.
1916	Menelik's son, Lij Yasu, deposed for his conversion to Islam and proposed alliance with Turkey; Menelik's daughter, Zauditu, becomes empress, with Ras Tafari as regent.
1923	Ethiopia joins the League of Nations.
1930	Zauditu dies; Ras Tafari crowned Emperor Haile Selassie I.
1936	Italians occupy Ethiopia; League of Nations fails to react.
1941	British oust Italians and restore Haile Selassie, who sets up a constitution, parliament and cabinet, but retains personal power and the feudal system.
1952	Eritrea, ruled by Italy until 1941, is federated to Ethiopia.
1962	Unitary state created; Eritrea is absorbed.
1972–1974	Famine kills 200,000 Ethiopians.
1974	Strikes and army mutinies against Haile Selassie's autocratic rule and country's economic decline; Derg stages coup.
1975	Ethiopia becomes a socialist state: nationalizations, worker cooperatives, and health reforms are enacted.
1977	Mengistu Haile Mariam takes power; Somali invasion of Ogaden repelled with Soviet and Cuban help.
1978–1979	Thousands of political opponents killed or imprisoned by the government.
1984	Workers' Party of Ethiopia (WPE) is set up on Soviet model.
1985	Live Aid concert raises funds to relieve famine caused by war and three years' drought.
1986	Eritrean rebels take control of the whole northeastern coast.
1987	People's Democratic Republic of Ethiopia declared with Mengistu as president.

1988 Eritrean and Tigrean People's Liberation Fronts (EPLF and TPLF) begin new offensives; Mengistu's budget is for "Everything to the War Front;" Ethiopia agrees not to interfere in Somali factional fighting and resumes diplomatic relations severed in 1977.

1989 Military coup attempt fails. TPLF in control of most of Tigray; TPLF and Ethiopian People's Revolutionary Movement form alliance, the EPRDF.

1990 WPE renamed Ethiopian Democratic Unity Party and opened to non-Communists; moves toward market economy begin; distribution of food aid for victims of new famine hampered by both government and rebel forces.

1991 Mengistu flees country in face of big advances by EPRDF and EPLF; EPRDF enters Addis Ababa and sets up provisional government, dividing country into 14 semiautonomous regions and promising representation for all ethnic groups; however, fighting continues between the mainly Tigrean EPRDF troops and various opposing groups; EPLF enters Asmara, the Eritrean capital, and sets up government.

1993 Eritrean independence is recognized.

1995 Transitional rule ends with multiparty democratic elections and establishment of a new nine-state federation. EPRDF, with a landslide victory, forms the first democratic Ethiopian government.

1998–1999 Border conflict with Eritrea develops into a serious and protracted war.

Further Reading

Blakely, Thomas D., Walter E. A. van Beek, and Dennis L. Thomson, eds. *Religion in Africa—Experience and Expression.* London and Portsmouth, NH: James Currey and Heinemann, 1994.

Connah, Graham. *African Civilizations.* London: Cambridge University Press, 1987.

DeVilliers, Marq, and Sheila Hirtle. *Into Africa—A Journey Through the Ancient Empire.* Toronto: Key Porter Books, 1997.

Iliffe, John. *Africans—The History of a Continent.* Cambridge: Cambridge University Press, 1995.

Bradshaw, Michael. *The New Global Order: World Regional Geography.* 2nd ed. New York: McGraw- Hill Higher Education, 2002.

English, Paul. *Geography: People and Places in a Changing World.* 2nd ed. St. Paul, MN: West Publishing Company, 1997.

Pulsipher, Lydia. *World Regional Geography.* New York: W. H. Freeman and Company, 2000.

Sager, Robert J., and David Helgren. *World Geography Today.* New York: Holt, Rinehart and Winston , 1997.

Salter, Christopher, et al. *Essentials of World Regional Geography.* 3rd ed. Orlando: Saunders College Publishing, 2000.

Index

Index

Picture Credits

About the Author

CAROL ANN GILLESPIE teaches World Regional Geography and East Asian Studies at Grove City College in Grove City, Pennsylvania. She resides in Cranberry Township, Pennsylvania, with her husband, Michael, and her three sons. She enjoys reading, writing, and travel, and loves when she can combine all three!

CHARLES F. ("FRITZ") GRITZNER is Distinguished Professor of Geography at South Dakota University in Brookings. He is now in his fifth decade of college teaching and research. During his career, he has taught more than 60 different courses, spanning the fields of physical, cultural, and regional geography. In addition to his teaching, he enjoys writing, working with teachers, and sharing his love for geography with students. As consulting editor for the MODERN WORLD NATIONS series, he has a wonderful opportunity to combine each of these "hobbies." Fritz has served as both president and executive director of the National Council for Geographic Education and has received the Council's highest honor, the George J. Miller Award for Distinguished Service.